TOOLS
AND
TIPS
FOR TODAY'S
PROJECT
MANAGER

TOOLS
AND
TIPS
FOR TODAY'S
PROJECT
MANAGER

Ralph L. Kliem
Irwin S. Ludin

PROJECT MANAGEMENT INSTITUTE

Library of Congress Cataloging-in-Publication Data

Kliem, Ralph L.
    Tools and tips for today's project manager / Ralph L. Kliem, Irwin
S. Ludin
        p.   cm.
    Includes bibliographical references.
    ISBN: 1-880410-61-3 (pbk: alk. paper)
    1. Industrial project management. I. Ludin, Irwin S. II. Title.
HD69.P75K595 1999
658.4'04 – – dc21   99–24030
                                                                 CIP

Published by: Project Management Institute Headquarters
                Four Campus Boulevard, Newtown Square, Pennsylvania 19073-3299 USA
                Phone: 610-356-4600 or Visit our website: www.pmi.org

ISBN: 1-880410-61-3

Copyedited by Jennifer B. Baumgartner

10 9 8 7 6 5 4 3 2 1

Dedication

To:
Tom, Doris, and Robert Thomas—RLK
Marlene R. Ludin—ISL

Contents

Figures

Tables

Preface

Being a project manager has never been more difficult than it is today. The work environment moves at a faster pace, and it demands more from everyone. Additionally, the technological tools change constantly, the customers demand higher quality of output, information requirements mushroom, and processes must be continuously refined and redesigned to improve performance and develop innovative solutions.

To aggravate the situation, you have only so much time, finance, skills, knowledge, power, and miracles to survive in this seemingly crazy environment. It would be nice to have some handy compendium of tools and tips readily available as a reference for helping you respond efficiently and effectively.

And you now have in your hands such a compendium. This book provides a list of common, and not so common, tools and tips to help project managers deal with eight categories of challenges that stretch their knowledge, abilities, and skills. For most project managers, the challenges they face daily fall within one of these categories. The eight categories, and their descriptions, are as follows.

1. Creativity—developing innovative solutions.

2. Information—converting data into a meaningful format.

3. Meetings—assembling people to achieve a specific goal.

4. Methods/processes—applying ways of doing business to transform input to output.

5. Organization—taking a structured approach for handling a host of situations.

6. People—addressing the human side of managing projects.

7. Planning—defining the whos, whats, wheres, whens, and whys of projects.

8. Time—making more of something that is becoming less available.

The TnTs in this book are arranged alphabetically. In the interest of helping you maximize the use of this book, however, each TnT is bucketed into one or more categories in the Appendix. To illustrate, if you need to handle a large volume of data, you can look in the Appendix under the information category to identify a TnT to help you. Perhaps you will select the affinity diagram or a statistical calculation like the mean.

If you need additional or more in-depth information on a topic, you can refer to the Bibliography for suggestions. It is divided into the eight categories and includes an additional general section; it also provides a listing of books that cover multiple topics.

Keep this book handy. It will provide you with the TnTs to work smarter, not harder. Although some of the TnTs appear to be commonsense, do not let overconfidence fool you. Many project managers could have done a better, smarter job if they had followed some of the simple steps suggested in this book. We have seen many project managers *go down in flames* because they did not construct a good outline. On the other hand, we have witnessed many project managers (including ourselves) who have applied the steps in this book and gained rich rewards as a result.

Tools and Tips

AFFINITY DIAGRAM

The affinity diagram is a technique for organizing a hodgepodge of items (e.g., ideas, facts). It is based on the notion that certain items share a commonality, such as a characteristic.

The affinity diagram offers two benefits. It brings simplicity to something that appears chaotic, and it furthers understanding of the relationships among the items.

 for Developing an Affinity Diagram

- Assemble the population of items.
- Identify the overall subject of the diagram.
- Develop the different categories and subcategories for the items.
- Place the items into the appropriate category or subcategory.
- Arrange the categories and subcategories into a hierarchical relationship.

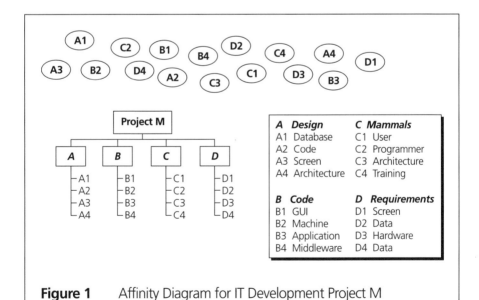

Figure 1   Affinity Diagram for IT Development Project M

AGENDA

An agenda is a prerequisite for an orderly meeting. If prepared correctly, it provides structure for a potentially mob-like situation. Remember, every meeting has the propensity toward disorder.

A good agenda has several characteristics. First, it covers topics meaningfully and logically. You should arrange your topics in an order that accomplishes the goal of the meeting. Just slapping topics on a piece of paper will not suffice; in doing so, you could address some topics, but not in a logical, meaningful order that would better accomplish the goal.

Second, it sets priorities. The agenda addresses the highest priorities first and then proceeds to the lowest ones. If insufficient time remains, you can address the lower priority items at the next meeting and not leave any serious outstanding issues.

Finally, it sets the time clock for a meeting. It paces a meeting so the entire session does not concentrate, for example, on one topic for fifty-nine minutes and on nine remaining topics for one minute.

 for Developing an Agenda

- Identify the overall topic of the session.
- Identify the subtopics that comprise the overall topic.
- Determine the most important subtopic, and list the remaining ones in decreasing order.
- Allot a specific time to address each subtopic, keeping in mind the total time available for the session.
- If necessary, assign responsibilities for each subtopic.
- Send out the agenda for preliminary review.
- Make revisions to the agenda.
- Distribute the agenda two to three days prior to the session.

ANALYSIS AND ANALYSIS PARALYSIS

Analysis is the process of breaking something down into its simplest components and identifying the relationships. A wide number of analysis techniques are available—from flowcharts to data flow diagrams.

Analysis offers advantages. It enables a simplified understanding of a process or object, furthers communication, and allows for experimentation. It also develops better ideas and products.

Sometimes, however, analysis turns into paralysis, meaning some people unceasingly refine the breaking down of components and identifying their relationships until, in their eyes, it is perfect. The result is that a long time transpires before action is taken, if any. Hence the term, *analysis paralysis*.

If not checked, analysis paralysis can lead to project delays, high frustration levels, and project costs.

 for Overcoming Analysis Paralysis

- Determine in advance the level of detail you want to achieve in describing a process or object.
- Set a time frame for how long the analysis can take place.
- Obtain input or feedback from people who know the subject or are in authority and can say, "It is done."
- Let the output of your analysis sit for awhile before revisiting it for modifications, and restrict the number of changes.

AUTHORITY

Most people can recognize authority, but they have difficulty defining it. Simply defined, it is having the power over people to accomplish some specific goal, objective, or task.

Authority comes from many sources and can fall into one of three categories: traditional, charismatic, and legal-rational.

Traditional authority is based upon what the term implies: tradition. Certain people have power over others based upon historical factors. A sheik in the Arab world has authority because he fills a position based upon historic precedence.

Charismatic authority is based upon innate personal qualities. Frequently, these people do not have any formal authority, only that granted by their followers. Martin Luther King, Jim Jones, and Huey Long are examples of people with charismatic authority.

Legal-rational authority is that given to a person by an institution. The degree of authority depends on one's position in the organization. Rank in the military is a prime example of legal-rational authority. Your boss at work is another example. Typically, the higher up in an organization, the more authority rests with a person.

In the business world, you can face a circumstance where a person holds a position that embodies two or three categories of authority. That's rare, but it translates into real power that can have positive or negative consequences.

Knowing who has what authority, and the basis for it, can help you. This information enables you to determine who makes decisions and the importance of those decisions. In other words, you can determine who are the *movers and shakers* in an organization.

TNT for Authority

- To determine the type of authority that exists in an organization, observe the following steps.
    - Look at the organization chart, identifying reporting relationships.
    - Identify who attends which meetings and who calls them.
    - Look for where the meetings are held.
    - Pinpoint who grants approvals for funding, taking action, and so on.
    - Pay attention to the formal and informal power structure.

BASELINING

Baselining is establishing what you release as the final output and using it to evaluate subsequent revisions. You can baseline reports, forms, plans, hardware, software, and many other items.

For example, you might have a report that will require many changes in the future. It is the document that everyone references when they must change it. You might designate the first report release 1.0 give each subsequent minor release a number like 1.1, 1.2, and so on, and each subsequent major release as 2.0, 3.0, and so on.

Baselining offers two advantages. First, it allows evaluating the impact of a change on your product. For instance, you can determine what aspects of your output will need altering and to what degree.

Second, it enables you to control changes. You can determine which changes are critical and can create a timetable to implement them.

 for Baselining

- Determine the characteristics of the item being baselined.
- Obtain consensus on what constitutes the item being baselined.
- If a change is necessary, analyze and evaluate the impact on the item.
- Give the item being baselined a version number.
- Keep separate versions for review and audit purposes.

Date	Subject	Version	Release Identification
January 2	Operator's Manual	1.0	Original Release
February 5	Operator's Manual	1.1	Incorporate equipment changes
May 11	Operator's Manual	1.2	Incorporate location changes

Table 1   Baseline Report for Project Z

BELL-SHAPED CURVE

The bell-shaped curve is also known as the normal curve of distribution. The concept behind the curve is that a sufficient number of randomly selected observations will fall in the middle, producing the shape of a bell.

The bell-shaped curve lays the groundwork for performing a host of statistical calculations. These calculations include sampling, probability, frequency distribution, and dispersion.

When actually taking the observations, the plotting of the observations may be skewed or asymmetrical. This reflects bias in the selection.

In a normal curve, the values fall within a specific area under the curve. For a normal curve, 68 percent of the values fall between +1 sigma; 95 percent, between +2 sigma; and 99 percent, between +3 sigma.

 for Developing and Using a Bell-Shaped Curve

- Obtain a frequency distribution.
- Determine the class intervals for grouping the data.
- Draw an x-axis (horizontal line) to reflect the intervals.
- Draw a y-axis (vertical line) to reflect the cumulate frequency of occurrence for each interval.
- Plot the frequency of occurrences.
- Determine the purpose of generating a bell-shaped curve.
- Determine the skewness.
- If the observations produce a skewed or asymmetrical curve, then use the median to determine the measure of central tendency.
- If the observations produce a bell-shaped or symmetrical curve, then use the mean to determine the measure of central tendency.

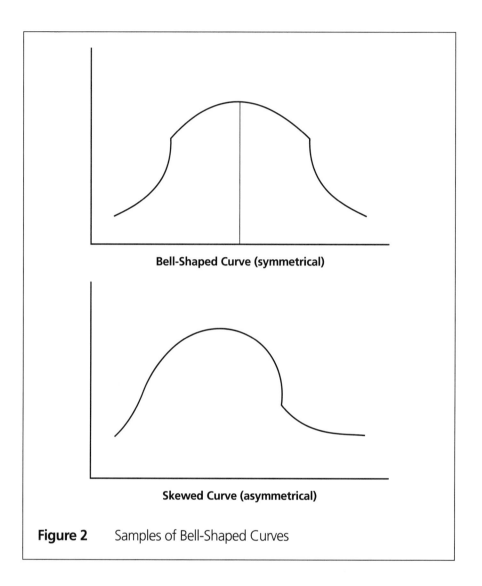

Bell-Shaped Curve (symmetrical)

Skewed Curve (asymmetrical)

Figure 2   Samples of Bell-Shaped Curves

BENCHMARKING

Benchmarking is a tool for identifying processes and comparing them to determine best practices.

The key to effective benchmarking is to use reliable, objective criteria when comparing and evaluating processes and practices. The criteria should be applied consistently.

Benchmarking provides three advantages. One, it identifies best practices. Two, it requires documentation of existing practices. Three, it encourages people to think about better ways of doing business.

 for Benchmarking

- Develop criteria for selecting firms.
- Develop criteria for comparing and evaluating firms.
- Determine the objectives of the benchmarking.
- Document the existing process.
- Remain consistent and objective when applying the criteria.
- Identify the best practices.

BRAINSTORMING

Everyone has the capability to create, say the psychologists and psychiatrists. The world, however, places constraints on creativity in the form of role-playing, norms, social mores, and laws. Thus, constraints inhibit creativity. History is replete with examples of people facing tremendous odds when attempting to create.

Brainstorming is a technique that will help overcome constraints and release creativity in people. It is an approach that engenders creative ideas from people by foregoing prejudices that lead to condemning any new idea.

 ## for Brainstorming

- Identify the topic.
- Identify the participants.
- Find a place isolated from distractions.
- Ensure the place is replete with supplies, equipment, and so on.
- When conducting the session, make sure no derisive comments occur.
- After identifying all the ideas, eliminate the nonvalue-added ones.
- With the remaining ideas, rank them from most to least important.
- Select the best idea(s) via consensus.

BREAKEVEN ANALYSIS

Breakeven analysis is determining when the costs of the existing product, service, and so forth, equal the costs of the proposed one. The point where the two costs equal each other is called the breakeven point.

The advantage of the breakeven analysis is to determine when the new product or service will be more economical than the existing one.

 for Performing a Breakeven Analysis

- Determine the costs for existing product, service, and so on.
- Determine the costs for the proposed product, service, and so on.
- Draw a graph to illustrate the relationship between the two, and identify the breakeven point.
  - Draw an x-axis to reflect the time continuum (e.g., months, quarters, years).
  - Draw a y-axis to reflect the cumulative costs.
- Draw a line reflecting the costs of the existing product, service, and so on, over time.
- Draw a line reflecting the costs of the proposed product, service, and so on, over time.
- Identify the point where the two lines intersect to determine the payback period.

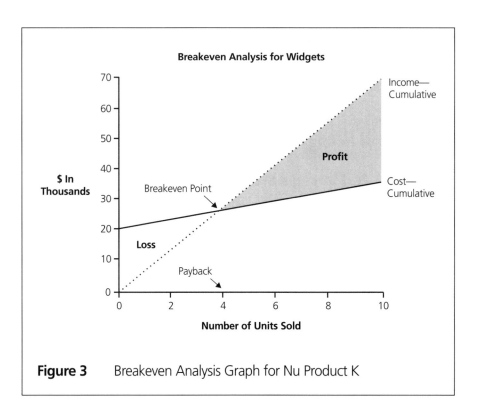

Figure 3   Breakeven Analysis Graph for Nu Product K

CAUSE-AND-EFFECT GRAPH

Analyzing today's business problems and distinguishing between causes and symptoms can prove virtually impossible. You have to sift through hundreds, even thousands, of pieces of information. Once you think you know the cause of the problem, you apply the treatment but discover that you've treated the symptom. So, you repeat this process until you've addressed the right cause.

Fortunately, a way exists to identify the causes of a problem that avoids repeating the process described above. It's called a cause-and-effect graph.

A cause-and-effect graph is a visual tool that reflects the interrelationships between causes and effects. You can then test each cause and effect to determine if a relationship exists.

Identifying causes and effects prior to implementing a solution saves you time and effort. You can pinpoint the cause of a problem and make the appropriate change rather than taking a SCUD-missile approach, which entails shooting at your target and hoping for a hit.

 for Developing a Cause-and-Effect Graph

- Identify all possible causes.
- Assign a unique identifier to each cause.
- Identify all the possible effects of each cause.
- Assign a unique identifier to each effect.
- Logically draw a line from a cause, or causes, to an appropriate effect.
    - Note: A combination of several causes may exist to create an effect.

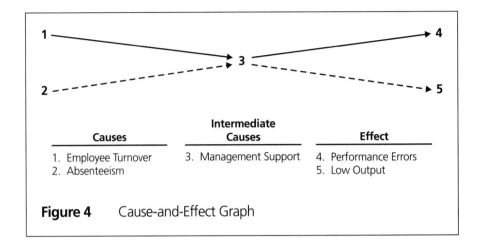

Causes	Intermediate Causes	Effect
1. Employee Turnover 2. Absenteeism	3. Management Support	4. Performance Errors 5. Low Output

Figure 4   Cause-and-Effect Graph

CHAIN OF COMMAND

The chain of command, also referred to as the formal *pecking order*, is necessary because it ensures coordination and communication among people in an organization. It also establishes who is reporting to whom.

Having a chain of command seems like commonsense to most business professionals. Yet many organizations operate without one. Inevitably, however, a chain of command does form, even if informally. This circumstance arises because emergent leaders (that is, those lacking formal authority) take charge by virtue of their skill, education, talent, or personality.

Establishing a formal chain of command in an organization or for your project will ensure continuity and engender responsibility and accountability.

If you're the head of a chain of command and you disappear for awhile, you can cause havoc because the *boss* is out. A smart approach is to assign a backup who acts on your behalf while you're gone. You can rest knowing that someone is *filling your shoes* while you do something else.

 for Developing a Chain of Command

- Identify the goals of your endeavor.
- Identify the people available to support you.
- Evaluate the characteristics (e.g., personality) and qualities (e.g., training) of the people.
- Select who will be the team leaders, keeping in mind span of control.
- Communicate the chain of command to everyone, perhaps through an organization chart.
- Support the chain of command throughout the endeavor.

CHANGE CONTROL SHEET

Think about the past. Have you ever developed something at work, like a report or software program, and as soon as you released it, you had to change it? More than likely, your answer is yes. More than likely, too, you needed a way to manage such changes. One way to manage changes is through a change control sheet.

The change control sheet records changes you released to your report, software, or product. You complete the change control sheet for each change and store completed sheets in a three-ring binder.

Each sheet should capture the source of the change and submission date, description, criticality, requested date change, disposition change, and actual implementation date.

The change control sheet offers two main advantages. It provides a historical record of changes made and offers you an opportunity to control changes and prioritize them.

Perhaps the biggest advantage, however, is that the change control sheet allows you to manage change rather than it manage you. You can then take a rational approach to handling change; that is, you can be proactive rather than reactive.

 for Developing a Change Control Sheet

- Identify the source for a blank change control sheet.
- Identify the destination for a double-sided change control sheet.
- List the essential information to be recorded on the sheet.
- Develop instructions for the sheet.
- Determine the desired number of copies of a completed sheet and what to do with them.

Source	Processing of Raw Material at Station 100
Submission Date	October 10, 19XX
Requested Date change	October 15, 19XX
Approved by / Date	M. Overseer / October 10, 19XX
Disposition Change	October 11, 19XX
Other Areas / Interfaces Effected	Purchasing (order quantity levels)
Remarks	None

Table 2   Change Control Sheet for Manufacturing Unit A

CHANGE MANAGEMENT

Nothing remains static, least of all a project environment. Change is common, and it is easy to react to it. A better way to approach change is to manage it. The way to do that is to establish policies and procedures for identifying and evaluating changes, whether to designs, requirements, documents, training programs, and so on.

The benefits of change management are threefold. First, it allows the project manager and the team to respond, rather than react, to changes. Second, it encourages anticipating the impact of a change and taking appropriate actions to minimize or preclude negative impacts. Third, it instills confidence in everyone that the project manager has control of the project.

Effective change management has three characteristics. First, it provides a means for placing changes into categories, such as major, minor, or corrective. Second, it provides a means for prioritizing a change; for example, it may determine whether a change is an immediate priority, minor priority, or not a priority. Third, it sets up a *change board*, usually consisting of two or more individuals. The purpose of the board is to categorize and prioritize changes, evaluate them, and decide their fate.

 for Change Management

- Select a medium for recording changes.
- Establish criteria for prioritizing changes.
- Establish criteria for categorizing changes.
- Establish a change board for categorizing, prioritizing, and evaluating changes.
- Document a change from identification to its eventual disposition.
- Document and communicate the change management process.

CHARTS AND GRAPHS

Charts and graphs are visual ways to display data. Some examples of charts and graphs include line graphs, bar charts, pie charts, histograms, flowcharts, and maps.

At a minimum, an effective chart or graph should be clear (that is, uncluttered and readable) and concise and should require little or no explanation. It should also include a title, legend, and date.

Charts and graphs provide many benefits. They can communicate information more effectively than text and can display information more compactly. They also ease analysis and evaluation.

 for Developing Charts and Graphs

- Determine the purpose.
- Define the audience.
- Determine the type (e.g., line graphs, bar chart).
- Prepare the chart or graph, ensuring clarity and conciseness.
- Add a title, legend, and date.
- If used in a presentation, ensure the audience can see and read it.

CHECKLISTS

Nobody can remember or think of everything. It is just one of our short-comings as human beings.

An excellent way to overcome that frailty is to develop checklists. A checklist is nothing more than a listing of items related to a particular subject. It serves as a reminder to perform some activity or to review something.

Checklists serve many purposes. They prevent oversights, especially for people with declining memories, and they ensure consistency of action if more than one person performs the action. They also prevent *reinventing the wheel*. That is, the items in the checklist are recorded and, therefore, are available to everyone with access to them long after the author departs.

You can use checklists for routine and nonroutine tasks or inspections. No matter what your profession (military, medicine, education, criminal justice, and so on), you can use them. You can also use checklists for any topic, including physical security, computing equipment, and facilities maintenance.

You can organize checklists in many ways. For example, you can arrange their contents chronologically, alphabetically, sequentially, or randomly. No matter how you organize checklists, however, you'll find that the time spent building them will never exceed the time saved using them.

 for Developing Checklists

- Identify the major categories of topics.
- List the categories in order of descending importance.
- Under each category, list items of relevance.
- Arrange the items within each category in descending order.
- Periodically review the checklist to determine your progress.

CHECKPOINT REVIEW MEETING

Sometimes, it pays to stop work, pause, and reflect on the progress you've made. You can then determine what did and did not go well. When working on a project, you can do the same thing through a checkpoint review meeting.

A checkpoint review meeting occurs at the conclusion of major tasks or phases in your project. You not only evaluate what did and did not go well, but you also decide whether to proceed or take a different approach.

 for Developing a Checkpoint Review Meeting

- Develop an agenda.
- Determine the date, time, and location of the meeting.
- Determine the topic(s).
- Identify the list of attendees.
- Gather input from the attendees about the date, time, and location.
- Take minutes of the meeting.
- Publish the minutes.
- Gather input from the attendees about the agenda.

CHUNKING

How do you stir-fry an elephant? Easy. You cut it up into manageable pieces. Unfortunately, many people do not fathom that concept. Instead, they take on a topic to write about in an article or manage a project that's so large they're doomed from the start.

Chunking entails dividing a topic, system, or just about anything else into varying levels of components and subcomponents. Chunking improves understandability, enables better tackling of effort, furthers traceability, and allows for easier assignments.

 for Chunking

- Take a *big picture* view of the subject.
- Determine the major components of the subject, paying close attention to natural divisions.
- Identify the relationships among the components.
- Identify what shared elements create relationships among the components (i.e., commonalties).

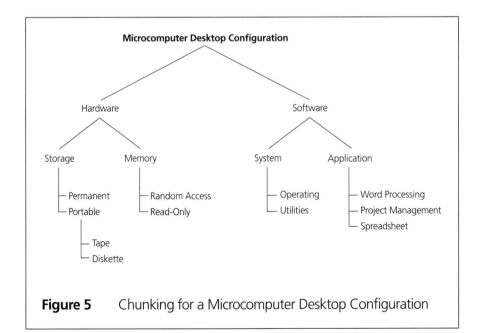

Figure 5   Chunking for a Microcomputer Desktop Configuration

COMMUNICATION DIAGRAM

Management experts have long speculated that two organizational structures exist in most business environments—formal and informal structure. The formal structure is reflected in an organization chart that displays the reporting relationships among individuals or business units. No such chart exists to reflect the informal power structure or the relationships that exist between individuals without the formal endorsement of management. However, you can identify and document informal relationships by developing a communication diagram.

A communication diagram shows the interactions, or level of communications, between two or more individuals in a specific setting, such as an office. It will help in identifying who communicates with whom.

The communication diagram helps you to determine the primary and secondary communications occurring in a workplace and to decide whether to change existing patterns. It also assists in determining where to apply technology that could enhance communication between individuals. Finally, it helps you identify political alliances and learn how to use them to your advantage.

 for Developing a Communication Diagram

- Identify all the major participants in the communication process on the diagram.
- Determine the length of time and the medium for monitoring communications among participants.
- Have the participants record their communications with each other.
- Compile the statistics.
- Generate conclusions from the data (e.g., areas for improvement).

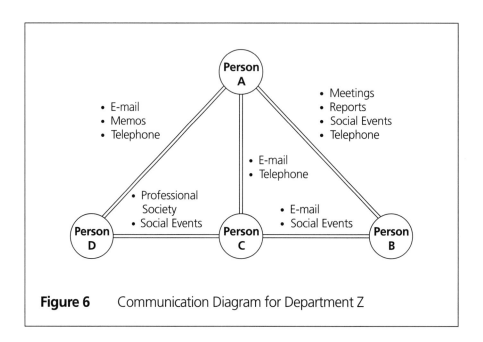

Figure 6   Communication Diagram for Department Z

Configuration Management

Configuration management is a formalized discipline for setting and managing changes to baselines. It falls under the rubric of change management.

A typical life cycle for configuration management observes the following steps.

1. Define the standards.
2. Document requests for changes.
3. Evaluate changes.
4. Record results.
5. Publish changes.

Good configuration practices require setting up an infrastructure to support all five phases of the life cycle for configuration management. These practices are set up early in a project and are followed throughout the project life cycle.

Configuration management offers many benefits. It reduces the opportunity for scope creep, and it controls costs and schedule slides via evaluation. It also provides an audit trail for analyzing causes to problems, developing lessons learned, and conducting project reviews and audits.

 for Configuration Management

- Establish cost, schedule, and performance baselines.
- Provide infrastructure for capturing and evaluating changes.
- Establish and follow procedures for configuration documenting and reporting.
- Maintain a good audit trail.
- Determine the standards for evaluations (e.g., contract terms).
- Follow accounting of configuration elements.
- Publish reports regularly.

CONFLICT MANAGEMENT

Conflict will always occur. It can exist between people and organizations. Unfortunately, it cannot be avoided and will always be present in some form. The key, however, is to manage conflict, but managing it is especially difficult between two or more people.

Conflict management, not conflict avoidance or confrontation, is a tool that can offer many advantages. It can help identify important issues and can cause resolution to occur. It can also spark new ideas for improvement and can generate enthusiasm for a particular endeavor.

 for Conflict Management

- Recognize that conflict is neither *good* nor *bad*.
- Keep *personalities* out of the conflict.
- Look at the *big picture*, and keep it constantly in mind.
- Maintain objectivity.
- Assess the facts, not the persons.
- Identify the cause of the conflict.
- Address the cause, not the symptoms.
- Seek consensus of the cause of the problem and the eventual solution.
- Monitor the situation, even after resolution of the conflict.

CONSULTANT SELECTION

Finding a good, reliable consultant can be *worth its weight in gold*. One challenge is that hiring a good consultant is difficult primarily due to a dearth of information about the person. Not surprisingly, the penalties for selecting the wrong one can be high and may involve disrupting the permanent workforce, incurring excessive charges, and applying incorrect advice.

Selecting a good consultant offers several benefits, including gaining invaluable advice and insights, accumulating productivity gains, and avoiding high overhead attributed to hiring permanent staff.

 for Selecting Consultants

- Ask for references and history.
- Select from a list of consultants.
- Avoid relying solely on cost.
- Consider personality attributes.
- Define clearly the service or deliverables or both.
- Conduct periodic review sessions with consultants.
- Know the terms and conditions of the contract.

CONTINGENCY PLAN

A contingency plan is a document, often a form, that captures anticipated problems, determines their criticality, and presents any appropriate responses. In other words, it is a method for *not getting caught with your pants down*.

You can develop contingency plans for just about any subject, such as for problems or circumstances related to people, equipment, supplies, facilities, money, and time.

Before beginning any project, consider completing contingency plans for every possible scenario and storing them in a three-ring binder. If a scenario arises that you failed to account for, complete a plan to help you take the right response in the future.

 for Developing a Contingency Plan

- Identify all the possible scenarios that can occur.
- Identify the most important scenarios according to predefined criteria.
- Determine the likelihood of occurrence (e.g., low, high) for each one.
- Determine the impact of each one.
- Determine the possible responses.

Description	Failure to Meet Service Levels
Criticality	High
Probability of Occurance	Moderate
Possible Responses	1. Temporary Agreement with Another Vendor 2. Hire In-House Staff
Consequences of Each Response	1. High Cost 2. Absorb Overhead

Table 3　Contingency Plan for Outsourcing Agreement

CONTRACT TYPES

Three varieties of contracts exist—cost-plus, fixed price, and time and materials.

The *cost-plus contract* requires payment of costs incurred for the service provided. In some circumstances, pure cost-plus contracts can be modified to include fixed, incentive, and award clauses.

The *fixed price contract* requires paying a specified amount for the service provided. In some circumstances, pure fixed price contracts can be modified to include escalation, redetermination, and incentive clauses.

The *time and material contract* requires payment for services using a specified labor rate (e.g., hourly) and materials cost.

A well-written contract offers three benefits. One, it prevents miscommunication between the major parties. Two, it prevents rework that results from misunderstandings. Three, it reduces the cost impact of fixes since the opportunity for rework has lessened.

 for Contracts

- Ensure that no ambiguities exist in the contract by clarifying all terms and conditions in writing.
- Prior to contract negotiation, determine requirements, particularly *must-haves* and *nice-to-haves*.
- Obtain solid, expert advice on legal and subject matters prior to signing the contract.
- Use the contract to develop the statement of work (or understanding).
- Periodically revisit the contract to determine compliance.
- Determine the risks associated with each contract type.

CONTROLLING

Controlling is ensuring that a project occurs according to plan. Of particular note are variances between what was planned and what has occurred.

There are several obvious advantages for controlling projects. One, it ensures effective accomplishment of goals and objectives. Two, it encourages more efficient accomplishment of goals and objectives. Three, it prevents crisis management from becoming a routine affair. Four, it enables consistent, realistic determination of priorities in a dynamic environment.

 for Controlling

- Hold frequent meetings with key participants.
- Keep a constant *finger on the pulse* of the project's performance (e.g., cost, schedule, quality).
- Maintain a project database to track and monitor performance.
- Apply good change- and problem-management techniques.

COST/BENEFIT ANALYSIS

In order to survive, the main goal of any business is, of course, to make money. To make money, however, requires spending money. Hence, it is important to know if an investment of money in a particular endeavor or product will generate a rate of return and, if so, when. This approach is called the cost/benefit analysis.

A good cost/benefit analysis has several characteristics. It lists all the major costs for the existing and new product, service, and so forth. These include costs for investments, implementation, and operations. It also includes a breakeven analysis, which determines when the costs of the existing product or service are equal to the proposed one.

Cost/benefit analysis contains a payback period, or the time frame in which the proposed product or service accumulates earnings to pay for itself. It has a rate of return that the proposed product or service is to earn after accounting for all costs. It also includes a net present value calculation, which is a discounted cash flow analysis using the present value of money. In other words, it accounts for the devaluation of money over time.

The benefits of a cost/benefit analysis are obvious. One, it helps to identify the value of an existing product, service, and so on. Two, it forces reevaluation of the current mode of doing business. Three, it encourages sound decisions.

 for Performing a Cost/Benefit Analysis

- Define the current and proposed product, service, and so on.
- List all major assumptions for the analysis.
- Calculate the investment, implementation, and operating costs.
- Perform a breakeven analysis.
- Calculate the payback period.
- Calculate the rate of return.
- Calculate the net present value.
- Perform the calculations for different scenarios.
- Evaluate the differences among the scenarios.
- List recommendations.
- Select the most appropriate recommendation.

Cost

Determining the cost of a product, service, and so forth, involves calculating a combination of three variables: investment, implementation, and operations.

The investment costs are the initial monies invested in the product or service to get it started, such as buying hardware. Implementation costs are costs incurred while getting the product or service implemented, such as labor. Operating costs are recurring costs, or those needed to keep the service or product available and ongoing.

Knowing the costs of a product or service enables calculating other formulas for a cost/benefit study, calculations that include the payback period and net present value.

 for Determining the Cost of a Product or Service

- Exactly define the product, service, and so on.
- Determine the elements that comprise each of the major cost categories (investments, implementation, and operating costs).
- Calculate the annual or cumulative costs.
  - For annual costs:

    $\dfrac{\Sigma \,(\text{Investment and Implementation Costs})}{\text{Life of the Product, Service, and so on.}} + \text{Yearly Operating Costs}$

  - For cumulative costs:

    Σ (Investment and Implementation Costs) + (Number of Years * Yearly Operating Costs)

    Where Σ means *the summation of*

CRISIS MANAGEMENT

Sometimes *all hell breaks loose*. Order turns into chaos. No one is in control. Sound familiar?

It should. It's called a crisis, and if you're not careful, it can overwhelm you. What you must do is handle a crisis in a manner that allows proaction rather than reaction. The way to accomplish this feat is through crisis management.

Typically, people react to a crisis. They implement a solution to satisfy short-term needs and treat the symptoms rather than the causes. Such reactions only quell the crisis instead of solving it, and they cause a crisis to reerupt later when the circumstances encourage it.

 for Crisis Management

- Remove the emotional content from the situation.
- Gather the facts and data of the situation.
- Look at the *big picture*.
- Define the problem.
- Identify the possible causes.
- Determine the true cause(s).
- Develop a solution that addresses the cause(s).
- Implement the solution.
- Seek feedback.
- Make revisions, as necessary.

CRITICAL ISSUES/ACTION ITEMS LOG

The critical issues/action items log is a form that you complete to record significant actions to perform in the future. Often, the entries are items not included in the work breakdown structure or schedule.

For each entry in the form, there are accompanying pieces of information: unique number, description, date assigned, actual completion date, priority, person assigned, suspense date, and comments.

The benefits of the log include raising visibility to the entries, generating commitment to resolving them, and serving as a record their completion or incompletion.

 for a Critical Issues/Action Items Log

- Identify the critical issues/action items.
- Write the items in the log.
- Archive the items over time.

Date: _____

Identifier	Description	Date Assigned	Person Assigned	Suspense Date	Actual Completion Date	Comments
001	Machine Q Critical to Delivery	January 3	Mr. Big	January 19	January 31	Recalculate Mean Time Between Failures

Table 4   Critical Issues/Action Items Log for Machine Shop L

CRITICAL SUCCESS FACTORS

When analyzing or solving a business problem, you cannot possibly understand every detail. You can only identify those functions, or processes, that affect the bottom line. These functions are called critical success factors (CSF).

To identify a CSF, you must ask yourself this simple question: If that function fails, will it affect the overall performance of the business? If your answer is yes, you can then concentrate on fixing or improving that function as opposed to the ones of lesser significance. After identifying CSFs, you also prioritize them when allocating resources. For instance, you give priority to CSFs when allocating time, money, supplies, facilities, and attention.

 for Determining Critical Success Factors

- Identify the main goal of your activity.
- Identify the processes or tasks for achieving the goal.
- Rank the processes in descending order according to importance in achieving the goal.
- Determine which processes need improvement, especially the most important ones.
- Implement the improvements.

DAILY PRIORITY TASK LISTING

The daily priority task listing shows all activities or tasks that you must complete on a particular day. Using this listing, you rank each task according to priority. For each task, you also set a tentative completion time. After completing each task, record your initial next to it.

The advantages to the daily priority task listing are many. Besides helping you manage your time and set your priorities, it also gives a historical record of your performance. This information will also help you evaluate your work performance and identify your accomplishments.

 for Determining the Daily Priority Task Listing

- Determine the overall goals to achieve for the day.
- Rank the goals according to descending importance.
- Set a certain time to accomplish the goal.
- Conduct a follow-up review with yourself to determine whether the goals, especially the most important ones, have been met.

Priority	Completed by	Task
3	4 P.M.	Status of Jigundo Account with Melissa
4	4 P.M.	New Office Furniture Resolution with Mike
2	3 P.M.	Budget Resolution for Next Quarter with Rick
1	Noon	Joint Merger with MeggaCorp (business plan) with Tonya

Table 5   Daily Priority Task Listing for My Corporation

DATA VERSUS INFORMATION

What we face today is data overload, not information overload.

The distinction is quite subtle but has a big impact on our lives. Data are facts and figures that have no meaning in themselves. Information, however, is data that are processed into some meaningful form. Hence, information is transformed data.

This distinction is important because many people confuse the two. How many times have you read a report filled with facts and figures that added little to the substance of the document? Or attended a presentation where the speaker provided slides and charts crammed with superfluous data? If the writer and speaker wanted to confuse you and others, they probably succeeded. If they wanted to communicate their message, then they probably failed.

Remember, what you and other people need is information, not data. Information, therefore, is useful, current, relevant, and meaningful. Data have none of these characteristics.

 for Managing Data and Information

- Identify what information you need and why.
- Identify what data are necessary to get the information.
- Organize the data according to some criteria or a criterion.
- Search the data for the desired information.
- Verify the accuracy of the information.
- Put the information into a comprehensible format.

DECISION-MAKING

"Decisions! Decisions! Decisions!" is the cry of people who loathe even the idea of making a decision. Yet, making a decision is not dreadful if you follow some simple guidelines.

First, avoid loss of objectivity. Second, distinguish between assumptions and facts, but if any doubt exists over whether a piece of information is a fact or an assumption, treat it as an assumption until you can confirm its status. Finally, recognize all constraints imposed on decision-making capabilities, such as schedule or budget, and, if doubt still exists, trust your intuition.

 for Effective Decision-Making

- Look at the *big picture*.
- Take the emotions out of the situation.
- Define the specific goal you want to achieve from the decision.
- Determine specific objectives that are based on the goal.
- Develop alternatives to achieve the objectives.
- Evaluate alternatives to achieve the objectives.
- Select the alternative for achieving each objective.
- Monitor performance in achieving objectives.
- Take corrective action, if necessary.

DECISION TABLE

A decision table eases decision-making. It is an illustrative tool used in handling the mass of information bombarding you when making a decision. It shows what actions to take in response to one or more conditions.

Basically, a decision table shows the conditions requiring action and the appropriate responses to one or more of those conditions. Decision tables are often used with—or in place of—procedures that address circumstances when many conditions exist that require a unique action.

 for Developing a Decision Table

- Identify all the conditions that might exist.
- Identify all the possible actions to take in response to a given set of conditions.
- Develop a table with the conditions listed in the top row and the actions listed in the left-most column.
- Where a condition intersects with an action in the table, determine whether the action should be taken (e.g., yes or no).

Rules	Less than or Equal to $1,000	Greater than $1,000
Conditions	Maintain existing contracts	Investigate new contracts
Actions		
Upgrade existing equipment	X	
Purchase new equipment		X

Table 6   Decision Table for Facilities Group

DECISION TREE

Decision trees make decision-making easier by identifying a series of conditions and actions.

They are used to determine actions in response to given situations. Sometimes decision trees become so long that you end up producing a voluminous number of pages. Some people use decision trees during planning sessions in a large room where they tape or paste the diagrams on a wall. Later, the decision tree is converted to a decision table for incorporation into a document.

One benefit of a decision tree is that it gives a visual depiction of all the conditions and actions of a decision. They are also easy to construct and follow, and they may be compressed into a decision table.

 for Developing a Decision Tree

- Identify all the conditions that might exist.
- Identify all the possible actions to take in response to a given set of conditions.
- Logically draw lines reflecting the sequence of conditions and the appropriate actions to take for each condition.
  - Note: Each condition should have at least two actions from which to choose.

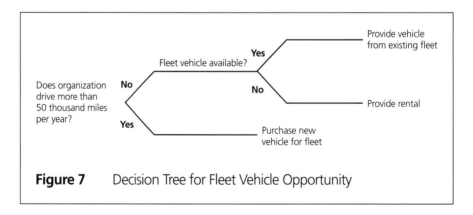

Figure 7   Decision Tree for Fleet Vehicle Opportunity

DELEGATING

Effective managers know how to delegate. They know how to allow people to manage and conduct tasks so they can concentrate on other matters.

Delegating tasks helps you and the delegatee. However, delegating is an art and requires will power on your part to make it work. Remember that you can delegate work but not responsibility. You are the one responsible for ensuring that the delegatee performs the task cost-effectively.

 ## for Effective Delegating

- Determine exactly what to delegate.
- Determine the desired results.
- Identify the desired characteristics of the delegatee.
- Communicate your expectations to the delegatee, offering assistance and providing sufficient information to do the job.
- Follow up periodically on the results being achieved.

DEMING WHEEL

Plan. Do. Check. Act. These are the four basic elements of the Deming Wheel for decision-making.

Plan determines what to achieve. *Do* executes the steps of the plan. *Check* obtains feedback. *Act* makes revisions. The wheel continues to turn, each spin lending a greater level of refinement.

A benefit of the Deming Wheel is that it is a simple model to follow. It also provides a model that leads to improved performance and is adaptable to a wide number of situations.

 for Applying the Deming Wheel

- Learn as much about the circumstances as possible.
- Determine what you want to achieve (*plan*).
- Execute the plan (*do*).
- Obtain feedback (*check*).
- Take corrective action (*act*).
- Continue following the wheel to refine the achievement of results.

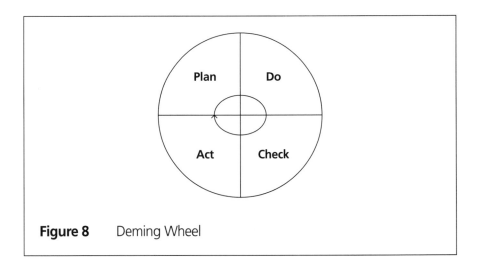

Figure 8   Deming Wheel

DESIGN PRINCIPLES

Design is the conceptual, functional, and physical structure of a system or product. In the past, designs were inflexible, offering the customer few options. Today, however, designs increasingly offer customers more options. The availability of these options is due to new, basic design-principles, which are helpful to anyone developing a process, procedure, product, or system—regardless of industry.

A *well-designed* item has several characteristics. It is highly modular, meaning that the parts are distinct components, and the interfaces between the components are standardized and simple. Key components make up the structural integrity of the overall item, and each part is defect-free prior to its union with the overall item.

Applying these basic design principles offers several benefits. The principles allow for reusability of components for building other processes, procedures, products, or systems. By allowing a *mix and match* capability, they also provide flexibility in responding to the customer's needs. Further, they not only guarantee a high level of quality through the use of tested parts, but they also allow the collection of metrics to measure quality and overall performance.

 for Design Principles

- Define the customer's requirements.
- Determine the overall components, keeping modularity in mind.
- Determine the interfaces between the components (e.g., exchange of data).
- Document the relationship and interfaces among the components.
- Ensure each component and its interfaces have been tested for reliability.
- Develop standard characteristics and formats for components and interfaces.
- Identify the key components and interfaces.
- Develop alternative designs for meeting the customer's requirements.

DIAGRAMMING

"A picture is worth a thousand words," once noted Confucius, the Chinese scholar. But there is a corollary that he failed to add: "And a picture shouldn't take a thousand words to explain." Yet too many pictures seem to follow the corollary rather than the Confucian wisdom.

The benefits of pictures are many. They communicate a lot of information in a short period of time, and they encourage questions that further clarify the message. They also prevent misunderstandings that often arise from text.

 for Effective Diagramming

- Provide a legend.
- Leave plenty of white space.
- Provide useful *header* information (e.g., title, date, page number).
- Do not use more than nine objects on a page; otherwise, it clutters the screen.
- Make the print legible.
- Use color sparingly, only to emphasize a point.
- Use symbols consistently.

DOCUMENT TEMPLATES

Many people frequently produce report templates or outlines of documents, and they complete the documents according to those outlines.

You can provide report templates in many ways. You can develop master copies of templates and have people photocopy them as needed. People can then complete the report according to the template. Or you can store the templates on a diskette and distribute the diskette to those who need it. People will then complete the applicable template and print the document.

Templates not only provide standardization and facilitate reading of reports, but they also reduce the chance of miscommunication. When using templates, people will find reports more readable due to the improved organization. Templates also save time because people do not spend time developing a document from scratch; they only fill in the details according to the organization of the template.

 for Developing Document Templates

- Identify the major segments of the document, usually consisting of an introduction, main body, and conclusion.
- Divide each segment into finer detail.
- Arrange the details within each segment into some logical order (e.g., spatial, time).
- Build the template using a word processing package.
- Use *cut and paste* to reuse parts of the template.
  - Note: Always archive the master file.

Travel Report	Medical Report
Date:	Date:
Name:	Name:
Employee #:	Address:
Address:	Social Security #:
Point of Origin:	Insurance Name:
Destination:	Malady:
Number of Days:	Diagnosis:
Total Cost:	Prognosis:

Figure 9 Document Templates for My Corporation

EARNED VALUE

Earned value is evaluating project performance via the relationships between cost and schedule. It uses three variables to evaluate performance:

- budgeted cost for work scheduled (BCWS)
- budgeted cost for work performed (BCWP)
- actual cost for work performed (ACWP).

These three variables are used to calculate cost variance (CV) and schedule variance (SV).

The cost variance is calculated using this formula:

$$CV = BCWP - ACWP$$

The schedule variance is calculated using this formula:

$$SV = BCWP - BCWS$$

A cumulative plot (see Figure 10) is generated for ACWP, BCWP, and BCWS. The differences between the plot lines for the BCWS and ACWP indicate the degree of cost variance. The differences between the plot lines for ACWP and BCWP indicate the earned value, or value of the work completed. The difference between the BCWS and the BCWP indicates the degree of schedule variance.

The schedule and cost variance can be converted into indices indicating (behind or ahead of) schedule or cost, respectively. A value greater than 1.0 indicates efficient schedule or cost performance. A value less than 1.0 indicates inefficient schedule or cost performance.

Earned value offers three benefits. One, it is a reliable tool for measuring the efficiency of a project from a cost and schedule perspective. Two, it can be generated easily through popular project-arrangement software programs. Three, it can be displayed in tabular or graphical form to show the relationship between ACWP, BCWS, and BCWP. However, earned value is not widely used, it requires some previous training or experience, and it involves self-discipline in employing consistent, valid status collection methods.

TNT for Using Earned Value

- Establish cost and schedule baselines for a project.
- Employ consistent, reliable status collection methods.
- Regularly plot or calculate the values for ACWP, BCWS, and BCWP.
- Use earned value to determine whether corrective action or replanning is necessary.

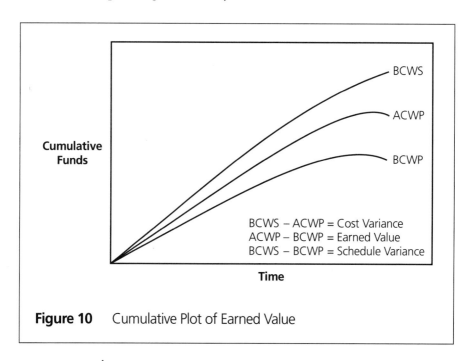

Figure 10 Cumulative Plot of Earned Value

EFFICIENCY AND EFFECTIVENESS

Efficiency is how much waste results from your activities. Ideally, you want to minimize waste to achieve high efficiency.

Effectiveness is how well you are achieving your goals. Ideally, you want to maximize the attainment of your goals.

Typically, the business world emphasizes efficiency. "Cut here. Cut there. Reduce expenditures by another 10 percent!" cries management. Determining the effectiveness of an organization often remains an abstract concept until year-end when performance assessment occurs. Then the assessment arrives too late; after the fact, everyone realizes what was efficient but not effective and vice versa. Indeed, sometimes the two can conflict.

Ideally, you want equilibrium between efficiency and effectiveness in whatever you do. Too much emphasis on efficiency results in *cheap and shoddy* performance. Too much emphasis on effectiveness can lead to wasteful expenditures. Seek moderation in achieving both.

 for Achieving Efficiency and Effectiveness

- Determine the overall goal of the endeavor.
- Identify the different ways to achieve the goals.
- Determine the desired levels of cost savings you want to achieve.
- Calculate the cost for implementing each alternative.
- Select the alternative that provides the desired level of cost savings.
- Determine the tasks to execute the selected alternatives.
- Put the tasks in a sequence.
- Take action by following the sequence of tasks.
- Monitor how well the tasks achieve the overall goal.
- Take corrective action, if necessary, by adding, deleting, changing, or resequencing the tasks.

E-MAIL

With the rise of distributed computing, Web technology, and groupware, E-mail has become a mainstay of business communications. Just about anywhere in the world, people can send and receive electronic messages, creating a global village in the truest sense.

E-mail offers several benefits. It communicates information quickly and efficiently and keeps communication open, even when senders and receivers are separated by great distances. It also allows people to budget their time (e.g., setting aside time to read, create, and send messages). However, the downsides to E-mail are its tendency toward information overload, spam (unwanted messages), and wading through superfluous messages.

 for Using E-mail

- Establish a set time each day to send and generate messages.
- Read or create the most important message first.
- Delete any unnecessary messages.
- Include source and destination when creating messages.
- When creating messages, practice principles of good business writing (e.g., clarity, conciseness, logic).
- Make backup copies of important E-mail messages.
- Respond to messages within a reasonable time (e.g., within twenty-four hours).

ENTROPY

Have you ever worked in an organization that lacked *energy?* One that seemed more interested in following its own internal rules and standards than operating to fulfill its reason for existence?

This organizational lethargy is called entropy, meaning that organizational energy has a tendency toward inertness. Performing functions becomes more important than achieving goals.

Entropy often occurs after an organization has achieved its goals in the past and then chooses to *rest on its laurels.* In other words, it *grows fat from prosperity.*

In this type of organization, implementing change—whether needed or not—becomes difficult. If you want to change a procedure, for instance, you will upset the status quo and face resistance from individuals or groups benefiting from entropy.

Change involves three types of people: *change agents*, people who introduce change; *change targets*, people who receive the change; and *change sponsors*, the high level people who endorse the change. All three play an important, interrelated role in successfully overcoming entropy in an organization.

 for Overcoming Entropy

- Develop a proposal for your idea by identifying the who, what, when, where, why, and how.
- Obtain top management support for your proposal.
- With any idea, start small and keep the scale manageable.
- Identify change agents, change targets, and change sponsors.
- Implement the idea(s).
- Monitor performance.
- Take corrective action, if necessary.

EQUIPMENT USAGE LOG

An equipment usage log tracks how and when equipment is, has been, and will be used. It is kept on a clipboard, or in a three-ring binder, next to the equipment and is completed daily. In the log, a person specifically records her name, the actual or planned start and stop dates (including time frames), and an explanation for using the equipment.

The equipment usage log offers several advantages. You know when people will use the equipment, and you and your colleagues can schedule your time accordingly. By reviewing earlier logs, you can also determine the extent to which people used the equipment and can decide whether additional equipment is necessary. Finally, you can determine whether people use the equipment for the right reasons.

 for Developing an Equipment Usage Log

- Identify the source for a blank log.
- Identify the destination for a completed log.
- List the essential information to be recorded on the log.
- Develop instructions for the log.
- Determine the desired number of copies of a completed log and what to do with them.

Name	Start Date	Start Time	Stop Date	Stop Time	Explanation
Melissa	November 7	2:30 P.M.	November 8	12 A.M.	Diagnostic Testing and Repair

Table 7   Equipment Usage Log for Machine Shop Y

FACILITATION (WORKSHOPS)

Facilitation is a key skill used in workshops that have a specific objective to achieve. Thus, it involves more than speaking before an audience. It also requires maintaining objectivity while simultaneously steering attendees toward a goal.

A well-facilitated workshop offers three benefits. It generates commitment to the results, produces consensus on major issues, and encourages information sharing and communications.

 for Facilitation (Workshops)

- Invite the right attendees.
- Remain objective and focused.
- Encourage participation from everyone.
- Ask a scribe to take notes.
- Follow an agenda.
- Obtain consensus on key issues.
- Establish *checkpoints* throughout the workshop to determine satisfaction of participants.
- Be prepared (e.g., have equipment and supplies available).
- Set up *parking lots* for issues you will return to later in the workshop.

FISHBONE DIAGRAM

Someone once said that nothing exists that cannot be improved. That statement has special relevancy when analyzing business practices to identify and remove problems. One way to accomplish this is by using the fishbone technique.

The technique requires assuming that you can analyze a major business problem by looking at four criterion: manpower, methods, material, and machines—the four Ms. For each criterion, identify problems associated with it. Then, determine what contributes to the major problem and develop the appropriate solution.

The benefits of the fishbone diagram are many. It is easy to prepare and encourages collaboration among all the people involved in the process being analyzed. It also serves as a basis for preparing procedures and is useful for analyzing a wide number of process problems.

 for Developing a Fishbone Diagram

- Draw a horizontal line through the center of page and then write a two- or three-word description of the problem.
- Determine criteria for evaluating the problem.
- Draw a line at an angle, and connect it to the horizontal line; repeat this until you have one line for each criterion.
- On each line for a criterion, record problems associated with it.
- Determine which smaller problems contribute to the overall major problem.

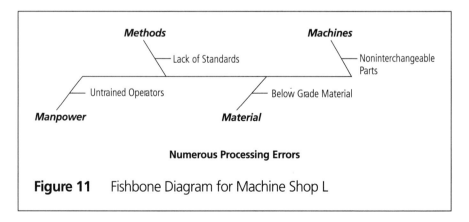

Figure 11   Fishbone Diagram for Machine Shop L

FIVE WS

The five Ws are who, what, when, where, and why. You can use the five Ws to find information when conducting research. For instance, you can use it to obtain information regarding an undocumented procedure or an event that has occurred. All procedures and events involve people, occur at a certain time and place, have a reason for existence, and accomplish something. Answering the five Ws helps you acquire that information.

You can obtain information that answers the five Ws in several ways. You can conduct interviews, develop questionnaires, or review documentation. Or you can combine one or more of the three methods. Armed with answers to the five Ws, you have sufficient information to make decisions or conduct further inquiry.

 for Defining the Five Ws

- Describe a situation, process, and so on, in one simple sentence.
- On a sheet of paper or using computer software, list the five Ws: who, what, when, where, and why. Be sure to leave enough space between each one to record information.
- For each W, record what you know and even what you do not know.
- For the latter, conduct follow-up questions to obtain the answers you need.

FLEXTIME

Flextime is providing variable working hours for employees, which allows them to arrive and depart from work within a window of time (e.g., plus-or-minus one or two hours). Everyone works a core set of hours, however, which ensures the availability of all people for a specific time period.

Flextime reduces absenteeism and overtime, and it increases morale and productivity.

 for Using Flextime

- Set guidelines for maximizing benefits.
- Establish core and variable hours.
- Track performance to determine whether productivity gains have been realized.
- Revise policies and procedures to reflect flextime arrangements.
- Emphasize that variable hours are for routine work.

8 A.M. – 9 A.M.	9 A.M. – 5 P.M.	5 P.M. – 6 P.M.
Flexible Hours	Core Hours	Flexible Hours

Table 8   Flextime Example

FLOWCHARTING

In the days prior to navigational equipment, pilots in monoplanes flew routes according to sketches. They would fly east, for example, looking at their hand-drawn map and at the ground. They would spot an object on the ground, such as a barn, and then would correlate it with what was shown on the map. The map might also direct the pilot to fly northeast for three minutes, looking for an open field with a light, and then land. In essence, the map was their version of a flowchart.

Flowcharts are essentially maps that illustrate the sequenced tasks and events of a procedure or process through the use of symbols. If you want to gather information for a flowchart, you can do it in two ways. You can interview people and sketch the flowchart as people speak, or you can take an existing narrative procedure and draw the flowchart while reading the document.

Flowcharts are easy to build. You can draw them by hand using a template or with a microcomputer equipped with graphics software. They are easily constructed, if not lengthy, and are easily followed. They also clarify points of confusion and use less verbiage to explain a process.

 for Flowcharting

- Identify the process to diagram.
- Draw the flowchart from left-to-right or top-to-bottom or both.
  - Note: Concentrate on sequence when drawing.
- Avoid putting too many symbols on a sheet. It is best to restrict the number of symbols to nine or less (excluding arrows).
- Provide a legend.
- Place a title and page number on each page.
- Ensure the print is legible.
- Use active verbs plus an object to describe what each symbol means.

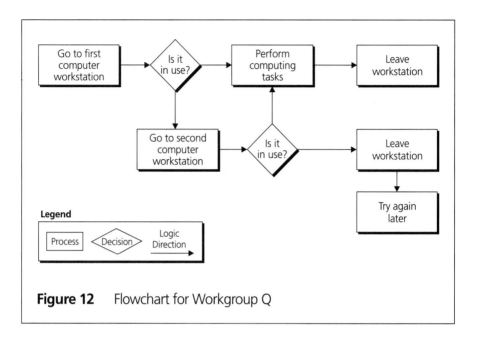

Figure 12   Flowchart for Workgroup Q

FORMS LAYOUT

Despite some people's dream of a paperless office, the reality is that forms are still present and have even proliferated in most offices. Like Gresham's law on money, the bad outweighs the good.

If you agree that forms will remain and increase in quantity, then you will agree that they should be well designed with the following characteristics. Forms must be clear and concise and should have a source and destination. They should also contain a completion date, instructions (other than "Fill in the information below"), logical field flow, approval section, form number, and latest issue date.

Forms are beneficial for capturing and retaining information. They also provide an excellent audit trail and are reproducible.

 for Forms Layout

- Determine the user of the form.
- Determine the people who will complete the form.
- Provide instructions for completing and submitting the form.
- Ensure that the form has a unique number and the latest issue date.

FREQUENCY DISTRIBUTION

Quite often, data come into the office in what seems like piles. Somehow, you must turn that data into information. Developing a frequency distribution is one way to do this.

A frequency distribution involves categorizing data and then determining how many occurrences appear in each category.

The frequency distribution quickly tells you how the data are distributed—that is, what categories hold the most data and which ones hold the least. You can convert the distribution into percentages by dividing the total occurrences into the subtotal for each category and multiply that figure by one hundred; the cumulative percent is one hundred.

Armed with these numbers, you can develop preliminary conclusions. You can determine what categories in the distribution have the most importance, assuming the categories with the most occurrences is indicative of those that are most important. You can also determine which categories are the least important and which categories might indicate an anomaly. Then, you can investigate further about the reason for their existence.

A frequency distribution offers several benefits. It gives you a *handle* on large volumes of data. It can also help determine patterns or trends and can facilitate decision-making.

 for a Frequency Distribution

- Develop criteria for stratifying data.
- Sort the data according to criteria.
- Plot the data to determine the norm and the anomalies, or calculate the norm to discover the anomalies.
- Draw conclusions from the information.

Machine Number	Number of Repairs per Year	Cost of Repairs per Year ($)	Cost per Repair ($)	Percentage of Total Repairs
1	1	100	100 (100/1)	10
2	3	450	150 (450/3)	30
3	6	1,200	200 (1,200/6)	60
Total	10	1,750	175 (1750/100)	100

Table 9   Frequency Distribution for Auto Body Shop R

GANTT CHART

In the early 1900s, an industrial engineer named Henry Gantt wanted to display—in calendar days—how long it took to complete a series of tasks. So he developed the Gantt chart, also called a bar chart, and scheduling has never been the same.

A Gantt chart is an illustration containing a series of bars showing the calendar, or flow time, for each task. Each bar begins on the left when it starts and ends on the right when it finishes. It may contain other information, too. For example, it may provide an activity description and names of people responsible for completing each task.

Although using the bar chart has become popular, it does have its shortcomings. It does not show dependencies or relationships among tasks—for example, which task comes first, then second, and so on. It also does not distinguish between critical and noncritical tasks.

Because of its shortcomings, the Gantt chart is not the best tool to manage the details of a project. However, if you want to communicate about schedules with higher management, then the bar chart is a good tool. With the bar chart, you can summarize your detailed schedules because management does not want all of the details, only summary information.

 for Developing a Gantt Chart

- Identify the tasks for your project.
- Determine the flow time for each task.
- Determine the start and stop time for each task, keeping in mind the sequence of each task.
- On the left side of the paper, list each task.
- Draw bars reflecting the flow time for each task, using the start and stop time for each task.

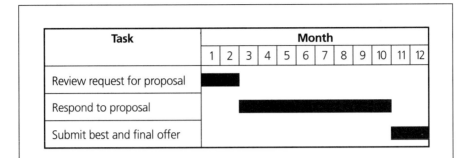

Task	Month											
	1	2	3	4	5	6	7	8	9	10	11	12
Review request for proposal												
Respond to proposal												
Submit best and final offer												

Figure 13   Gantt Chart for Response to Proposal for
Company XYZ

GLOSSARY

In an age of specialization, communication can prove difficult among people working on a project or within an organization. Some people use similar terms which have different meanings, and other people use esoteric terms that even experts in the field don't understand! If you're in charge of an organization or a project, you might consider developing a glossary.

The glossary need not be exhaustive. It might contain definitions of terms and acronyms that few people know or understand or are only particular to your environment. You can include the glossary as part of an administrative or technical manual or as a stand-alone in hard copy or electronic media form. If you don't want to develop a glossary, then you might consider purchasing and distributing a technical dictionary that everyone can reference.

A glossary offers two advantages. It helps to reduce miscommunication and misunderstanding, and it provides a convenient way for people to find definitions rather than wasting time developing or seeking one.

 for Developing a Glossary

- Identify terms that are used in a text (e.g., user manual).
- Develop new definitions, or use existing definitions, keeping in mind not to use the term in the definition itself.
- Arrange the terms in some order (e.g., alphabetical).
- Highlight the term (e.g., boldface or italics) for ease in locating it.
- Limit the definition of the term to no more than two sentences.

GOALS AND OBJECTIVES

Contrary to popular belief, goals and objectives are not the same. Goals are statements or descriptions of intent that describe what to achieve in the future. They are broad rather than specific. An example is: "Build a world-class product."

Objectives, on the other hand, are specific, measurable items that tell whether the goal has been achieved. One or more objectives lead to the achievement of a goal or several goals. An example is: "Build software modules with a level of quality that is no less than six sigma."

The advantages of goals and objectives are threefold. One, they provide unity of direction for an organization (e.g., company, project team). Two, they provide an ability to track progress. Three, they provide a means for determining the effectiveness of work.

 for Developing and Using Goals and Objectives

- Define the overall goals you want to achieve.
- For each goal, list the objectives.
- Ensure that all people involved with the attainment of goals and objectives provide input.
- Develop measurements to determine how well the objectives are being met.
- Consistently take measurements to track progress.
- Publicize the goals and objectives.

GROUPING

Many people allow themselves to become swamped by details, thereby letting themselves make life more complex than it really is. Some people look for ways to simplify life. One way to achieve simplicity is through a process known as grouping.

The grouping process begins with a person looking at nonsensical data and deciding to make some logical sense of it. This person takes the datum and groups it into logical components, i.e., good versus bad data. Having grouped the data, he then tries to extrapolate the relationships between those groupings.

Grouping offers several benefits. It reduces complexity and avoids analysis paralysis. It also facilitates identification of patterns and creates an order out of the data.

 for Grouping

- Determine the overall *boundary* of the data being analyzed.
- Develop some artificial criteria for categorizing the different elements of what falls within the boundary.
- Group the elements according to the criteria.
- *Flag* those elements that do not fit within a category.
- Develop a unique category for the anomalies, or remove them.

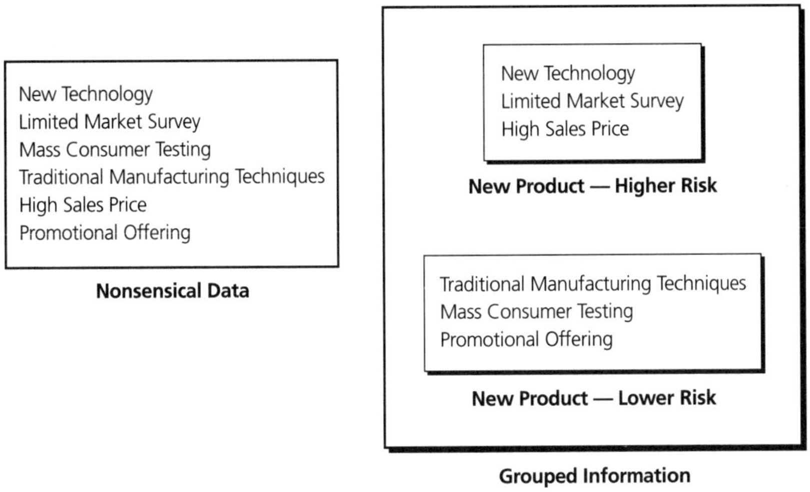

New Technology
Limited Market Survey
Mass Consumer Testing
Traditional Manufacturing Techniques
High Sales Price
Promotional Offering

Nonsensical Data

New Technology
Limited Market Survey
High Sales Price

New Product — Higher Risk

Traditional Manufacturing Techniques
Mass Consumer Testing
Promotional Offering

New Product — Lower Risk

Grouped Information

Figure 14   Grouping for Nu Product Corporation

HEURISTICS

Heuristics are simply *rules of thumb* for dealing with a given situation. They are beneficial when time and money are not available for conducting an in-depth analysis. They are based on the concept of generalizations; when action needs to be taken, generalizations are made about a given item and situation.

Heuristics are quick, inexpensive, and effective. The downside is that applying the wrong heuristic can have negative and unforeseen consequences.

 for Heuristics

- Identify the major elements of an item or situation.
- Identify the fundamental relationships among the elements.
- Define the problem or situation in a simple sentence.
- Determine the goal of applying a heuristic.
- Anticipate positive and negative consequences, and make preparations to capitalize on the positive and manage the negative.

HISTORY FILE

A project history file is a way to keep records and data. Such information is then easily referenced when planning for the future and analyzing the past.

Kept in a manila folder or an electronic file, a project history file contains documentation about a specific project. Just about anything can go in the folder, including original and revised documents. Some documents to include are schedules, minutes, budgets and expenditure records, memorandums, statistics, reports, and completed forms.

The key to having a useful project history file is to update it regularly and organize the contents logically. A history file will be of no use to you or anyone else if it contains partial information or if its contents look like a swirl of paper.

Keeping a history file provides several advantages. You can clarify any ambiguities and answer any questions. You can also trace the progress of your project. Finally, you can transfer your project to someone else with minimum difficulty because the other person can read the file and can start on the project early.

 for Developing a History File

- Identify the topics to retain in documentation (e.g., schedules, budgets, forms, memos).
- Prepare a file for each topic.
- Label each file.
- Logically organize the sequence of files.
- Periodically purge the files for dated or irrelevant material.

HYPOTHESIS FORMULATION AND TESTING

A hypothesis is nothing more than a statement that requires verification. Hence, it remains speculation until tested. Hypotheses are useful for verifying inferences from data and for determining the differences between observations and expectations.

A hypothesis has two parts: the null hypothesis (Ho) and the alternate hypothesis (Ha). The null hypothesis is a negative statement while the alternate hypothesis is phrased positively.

A problem with having a null and alternate hypothesis is that an incorrect conclusion can be drawn, also known as an inferential error, from a sample. There are two types of these errors: type I and type II. Type I occurs when the null hypothesis is rejected even though it is, in fact, true. Type II occurs when the null hypothesis is accepted even though it is, in fact, false.

A common approach for testing a hypothesis is the test of significance. Basically, this entails assessing the degree of difference between the null and the alternate hypothesis. The difference is then assessed to be significant or insignificant. The probability of one of the differences being more wrong than the others is called the significance level. The degree of certainty is the confidence level.

There is one major benefit of hypothesis formulation and testing. It provides a means for testing inferences so that decisions can be made without relying on false assumptions.

 for Hypothesis Formulation and Testing

- Define the null and alternate hypothesis.
- Determine the desired confidence level or level of significance.
- Determine the sample size.
- Calculate the differences between the expected and actual results.

IMAGINEERING

Imagineering is picturing in your mind what you want to do or create and then introducing it into the *real world*. Simply create a mental image, in ideal form, of what you hope to see, remembering every detail; then, introduce the ideal into the real world.

Naturally, reality will hit you in the face. What is produced in the real world looks different from the ideal because the limitations of your capabilities to impose the ideal will soon surface. Some frustration, anger, and disillusionment often surface no matter how well the person performed imagineering.

Nonetheless, imagineering allows you to define what you hope to achieve and what will be required. It also anticipates the difficulties you may encounter, and it permits you to experiment in your mind with what the ideal will look like before you actually take action, which saves time, effort, and resources.

 for Imagineering

- Find a quiet area and sit down.
- Formulate in your mind the *perfect* image of the desired object, circumstance, and so on.
- Let the image take different forms.
- Select the image that best captures your wants and needs.
- Plan for implementing the image.
- Execute the image.
- Take corrective action.

IMPACT ANALYSIS

Changing an information system or an organization can have varying impacts. One way to assess the magnitude of a change is to conduct an impact analysis.

An impact analysis involves defining a change and determining its affect on the current mode of doing business. It requires assessing a change from three perspectives: technical, operational, and economical.

A *technical perspective* assesses change by looking at the ways it modifies a system. An *operational perspective* assesses change by looking at the ways it modifies a process or procedure. An *economical perspective* assesses change by looking at the financial affects of the change.

Conducting an impact analysis offers two benefits. One, it enables proaction rather than reaction to change, and two, it helps in managing the introduction of a change.

 for Conducting an Impact Analysis

- Define exactly what the change is.
- Determine the technical impact of the change.
- Determine the operational impact of the change.
- Determine the economical impact of the change.
- Prepare an impact analysis document.

I. **Description of Proposal Change**

II. **Description of Current Environment**
   A. People
   B. Processes
   C. Procedures
   D. Tools
   E. Constraints

III. **Technical Impact**
   A. Hardware
   B. Software

IV. **Operational Impact**
   A. Resources
   B. Procedures
   C. Schedule

V. **Economical Impact**
   A. Costs
   B. Breakeven Point
   C. Return on Investment

Figure 15   Example of Table of Contents for an Impact Analysis Document

INFORMATION CENTER

An information center is a central place where people go to acquire or communicate information. Often, it is a place where considerable pedestrian traffic occurs, such as coffee rooms, break rooms, copy centers, and company libraries. It contains many items of informational value. For instance, an information center might include newsletters, bulletins, memos, documents, policies, procedures, videocassettes, or audiocassettes. It might also contain blank copies of commonly used forms.

In addition to informative media, an information center can have useful equipment and furniture. For instance, it might have a whiteboard or bulletin board for recording or hanging messages. It might also have audiovisual equipment for people to use or borrow temporarily.

Because it serves as a communications hub for employees, an information center must be updated regularly. Otherwise, people will not have confidence in it.

The advantages of an information center are twofold. It is a convenient place to compile and distribute important information, and it is a place to clarify misunderstandings or stop rumors.

 for Setting Up an Information Center

- Identify the overall goal of the information center.
- Identify the different ways to present information.
- Determine its location.
- Determine the topics to cover.
- Determine the needed equipment, supplies, facilities, and so on.
- Keep the information center updated regularly.

INPUT-PROCESS-OUTPUT ANALYSIS MODEL

In business, one way to understand your environment is to use the input-process-output (IPO) analysis model. The model rests on the assumption that business entities (such as firms, offices, and plants) use inputs, perform processes, and produce outputs to sustain themselves and to expand.

Inputs might include nonlabor resources, manpower, data, and money. Processes, which transform inputs into output, include functions, actions, and operations. Outputs, which are the results of processes, include products, information, and reports.

The IPO analysis model offers many advantages. Viewing a business in terms of the IPO analysis model enables seeing the interrelationships of all the activities in a business from various perspectives, such as managerial or labor. You can also see the relationships among all the different people or organizations in a business.

Using the IPO analysis model also reduces the complexity in understanding how an organization operates. It simplifies reality by breaking your business environment into three components—inputs, processes, and outputs—and identifying the interrelationships among them.

 for Developing an Input-Process-Output Analysis Model

- On a sheet or paper or using computer software, list all the processes that can occur for the entities being analyzed.
- On the left of each process, list the inputs that feed it.
- On the right of each process, list the outputs that feed it.
- For a process that either receives or feeds other processes, draw a line between them to reflect that relationship.
    - Note: Label the line to describe what is being transferred between the processes.

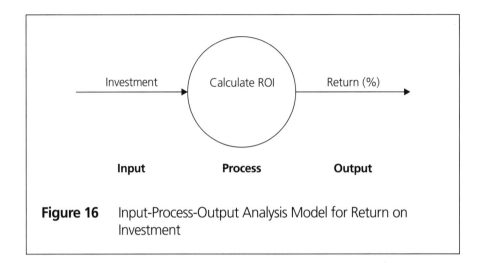

Figure 16   Input-Process-Output Analysis Model for Return on Investment

INTERRUPTION REDUCTION

In today's business world, finding time to work quietly can be an impossible task. Interruptions constantly enter your office from different sources—the intercom, the telephone, the secretary, your colleagues, the janitorial service. Small wonder you get any work done at your office. Yet it's not a lost cause. Through perseverance, you can acquire time to do your job.

The advantages of reducing interruptions are obvious. You can focus your concentration, set and address priorities, and increase productivity.

 for Interruption Reduction

- Keep your door closed during certain times of the day.
- Put your phone on call forwarding, or have voice mail or a secretary screen your calls.
- Choose an isolated place in your building to work.
- Work at home, if possible.

INTERVIEWING

Most people do not have the interviewing skills of a seasoned professional. Yet you do not have to be a seasoned professional to conduct a decent interview—if you know what to do.

Because interviewing is not easy, you need to plan in advance for the interview session by doing research. During the interview, you need to avoid influencing the interviewee to mimic what you want to hear. You need to prepare yourself.

Interviewing offers several advantages. It enables you to gather a large volume of information over a short period and gives you insights into a topic that you would not ordinarily discover. It can also lead to further sources of information.

 for Effective Interviewing

- Determine the goals and objectives that you want to achieve during the interview session.
- Collect as much background information prior to the session to familiarize yourself with the interviewee and the subject.
- Determine the approach to questioning (e.g., structured, unstructured).
- Set the date, time, and location far enough in advance for both you and the interviewee to prepare.
- Create a positive atmosphere, keeping the interview free from distractions, disruptions, and face offs.

Issue-Action Diagram

In the business environment, analyzing a situation or circumstance often involves multiple issues rather than a single one. Unraveling the complex relationships can prove trying. However, an issue-action diagram can help simplify the complex arrangement.

The issue-action diagram is essentially a decision tree that logically flows from left to right. It uses a series of branches to determine the most appropriate action to take.

An issue-action diagram offers several advantages. One, it provides a better understanding of a situation via simplification of the relationships among issues. Two, its simplicity allows for better communication with those affected by the issues. Finally, it is easy to develop.

 for Developing an Issue-Action Diagram

- List all the issues involved, being sure to thoroughly define each.
- Write each issue in the form of a question that reflects a choice of action, or write it in the form of a declarative sentence when a choice is not applicable.
- Identify the logical relationship between the issues, and record that relationship.
  - Note: Use arrows to reflect the direction of the relationship.
- Once the linkages of the issues are complete, determine the appropriate actions to take.
- Verify the accuracy by obtaining feedback from the people affected by the issues.

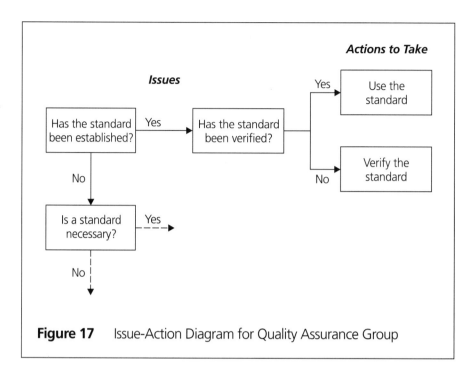

Figure 17 Issue-Action Diagram for Quality Assurance Group

Tools and Tips for Today's Project Manager

JUST-IN-TIME DELIVERY

Just-in-time (JIT) is a delivery approach for materials. Although used in the manufacturing arena, it is applicable to other environments, including service industries.

JIT is predicated on the following principles.

- Small lot sizes are better than carrying large inventories.
- Waste is negative.
- Long setup times are bad.
- Quality is important.
- Reliable production schedules are necessary.
- Good customer-supplier relationships are important.
- Employee involvement is critical.

JIT offers many advantages. It keeps inventory low, reduces inspection costs, and streamlines product or service delivery processes. It also solidifies relationships with users and improves quality. Further, it emphasizes a *pull* (customer-driven) rather than *push* (manufacturer-driven) provision of services.

 for Just-in-Time Delivery

- Prepare for cultural change.
- Develop reliable production schedules.
- Institute reliable, quality measures (e.g., statistical process control).
- Establish a good working relationship with suppliers.
- Obtain the involvement of people affected by the JIT delivery system.
- Keep order quantities small.
- Track performance of processes.

KEY CONTACT LISTING

A key contact listing presents the names of people that you feel are important in meeting your needs. You might place people on the listing for many reasons, including knowledge, skill, personality, wisdom, or physical prowess.

A key contact listing offers several advantages: other people can refer to it, you don't have to depend on other people to find out who's who, and you can retain the knowledge of who's who even after the person with that information departs.

You can build the key contact listing using a word processing, spreadsheet, or database package on a microcomputer. You can alter the data as changes arise, and then can reprint and distribute it. If you do not have a microcomputer, you can record the information on index cards and store them in a cabinet.

 for Developing a Key Contact Listing

- Identify the key people that can affect your performance.
- For each person, list their name, title, location, phone number, E-mail address, organization, and any background information that may be of use.
- Organize the listing of key contacts according to some criteria or a criterion (e.g., expertise).
- Frequently update the listing.
- Make it a point to occasionally contact these people, whether to verify the information or to renew ties (e.g., networking).

Name	Title	Location	Phone Number	E-mail	Organization
Jim	Chief Financial Officer	Building 5	x-3456	jim@jigundo	20
Bill	Chief Information Officer	Building 3	x-5678	bill@jigundo	30
Fred	Chairman of the Board	Building 6	x-1000	fred@jigundo	10

Table 10   Key Contact Listing for Harry Jones

Tools and Tips for Today's Project Manager

LEADING

All projects require leadership. Without good leadership from the project manager, the chances of a successful outcome are diminished. Leadership involves inspiring people to perform in a manner that meets or exceeds requirements. But how does a project manager do that?

Leaders provide a vision—that is, they communicate to people a solid visualization of the end result. They also provide a path for achieving the vision. Of course, developing a vision and a path, albeit important, is not enough. They also must generate a sense of urgency and enthusiasm for accomplishing the goal. Further, they must generate in people a sense that the project's goal is their own goal and that the path is their path. Above all else, they must sustain interest via communication and maintain everyone's focus.

Leadership offers three obvious benefits. One, it results in greater productivity than the sum of the individual parties, often called synergy. Two, it encourages greater cooperation among all the participants. Three, it terminates with the effective and efficient achievement of goals and objectives.

 for Effective Leading

- Define the goals and objectives of the project.
- Develop a path to achieve the goals and objectives.
- Encourage ownership in the goals, objectives, and path.
- Constantly communicate the goals, objectives, and path.
- Track and monitor progress in achieving the goal.
- Place as much importance on the *soft skills* (e.g., active listening, interpersonal relations) as the *hard ones* (e.g., scheduling, finance).

LESSONS LEARNED

A lessons learned is a document, in essay or bullet-list form, that notes what did and did not go well on a project.

It should contain an overview of your project and a listing of major activities and should describe what went positive, what went negative, and why for both. It should then be distributed so people truly learn the lessons, and it should not be filled with platitudes and self-promotion.

The lessons-learned document helps you to learn from your mistakes and appreciate your successes. It also has other benefits: it keeps you from repeating mistakes and helps others to avoid them too.

 for Lessons Learned

- Develop an outline of the lessons-learned document.
- Contact people for their input on relevant topics.
- Compile the input.
- Draft the document.
- Circulate the document for review.
- Incorporate revisions.
- Distribute the document to the appropriate people.

---

1. Description
2. Scope
3. Organizational Structure
4. Schedule Delivery
5. Cost
6. Project Successes
7. Project Shortcomings
8. Approaches/Directions Using Hindsight
9. Recommendations
10. Conclusions

Figure 18   Lessons-Learned Document for Project XX

LISTENING

In today's high-technology environment, we are continuously barraged with noises from people and machines. After awhile, we become desensitized to the noise, commonly called *tuning out*. We still hear, but we stop listening. This can start affecting our work performance—all the more reason to have good listening skills. However, listening requires great discipline.

Listening is advantageous because it enables collecting a large amount of information. It also enables determining what is and what is not important. Finally, it avoids misunderstandings, and it builds *bridges* rather than *walls*.

 for Effective Listening

- Focus on the message, not on the individual.
- Avoid making distracting mannerisms or comments.
- Maintain eye contact.
- Use expressions that communicate you are listening.
- Do less talking and more listening.
- Empathize, don't sympathize.

MAKE-BUY ANALYSIS

The make-buy analysis determines whether to purchase or build a product. It involves looking at different alternatives and using cost, schedule, and quality criteria. For cost, the key criteria are development and sustaining costs, payback period, and the time value of money. For schedule, the key elements are times for building and delivering the product. For quality, the key elements are reliability, repeatability, and maintainability of the product.

Make-buy analysis offers two benefits. It precludes embarking on inefficient and ineffective projects, and it provides a basis for good contract negotiations and planning.

 for Make-Buy Analysis

- Define the objective or specifications of the product.
- Determine the different alternatives to pursue.
- Determine cost, schedule, and performance requirements to evaluate alternatives.
- For each alternative, apply requirements.
- Select the best alternative that satisfies the objective(s) or specification(s).

MANUFACTURING RESOURCE PLANNING (MRP II)

MRP II is a comprehensive, integrated system for managing the resources of a corporation. It includes processes from business planning to scheduling with suppliers. Actually, MRP II is the successor to material requirements planning (MRP), which is more narrowly focused and considers mainly production scheduling, bills of material, and requirements.

Increasingly, MRP II is used with just-in-time techniques because MRP II focuses more on satisfying the quantitative requirements of work orders than on quality. Together, quantity and quality are satisfied.

MRP II offers many benefits. It reduces the need to keep excess inventory. It also encourages better planning and teaming among all the players. Finally, it encourages improved satisfaction of customer requirements.

 for MRP II

- Establish and integrate processes, from business planning to production scheduling.
- Encourage teamwork among the process owners (e.g., engineering and design).
- Document the MRP II system.
- Ensure production control and scheduling disciplines are in place.
- Ensure controls exist to preclude inventory excesses and shortages.

MATRIX

A matrix compactly displays the interrelationship between two or more datum. Many business professions use matrices. Auditors develop them to identify the relationships between threats and controls. Systems analysts develop them to identify the relationship between inputs and outputs for a computing system. You can use them, too, for many purposes, especially to display relationships in a compact chart.

Matrices offer several advantages. They enable displaying a large amount of information in a compact form. They are also easy to prepare and show relationships among pieces of information. Finally, they provide a good basis for making decisions.

 for Developing a Matrix

- For one set of data, identify the number of rows reflecting the number of entries in the matrix.

- For another set of data, identify the number of columns reflecting the number of entries in the matrix.

- Draw a large rectangle.

- Draw the appropriate rows and columns in the matrix.

- Develop a set of symbols to reflect the type or strength of the relationship.

- In each row, place the appropriate symbol to reflect the type or strength of the relationship.

Activity	Monday	Tuesday	Wednesday	Thursday	Friday
Prepare presentation	X				
Presentation dry run			X		
Deliver presentation					X

Table 11   Matrix for Presentation to Jigundo Corporation

MATRIX VERSUS TASK FORCE STRUCTURE

There are two basic organizational structures for most projects: matrix or task force.

A *matrix structure* is used when resources from various functional organizations work on multiple projects. This structure offers the benefit of sharing resources, especially among people with a rare expertise. It also provides management the flexibility to cease projects and start new ones without having to hire and fire people. Its principal downsides are burnout and conflict over resource usage.

The *task force structure* is used when resources from various functional organizations work full-time on a project. The task force structure offers the benefits of visibility, concentration of effort, and experimentation. Its principal downsides are loss of commitment to a project, and later in its life cycle, declining morale.

 for Determining Whether to Use Matrix or Task Force Structure

- Determine the availability of resources with the requisite skills.
- Determine the desired level of organization *flexibility*.
- Determine the historical precedent for using matrix or task force structure for the type of project.
- Determine the desired degree of autonomy for the project team.
- Determine the desired level of visibility for the project.

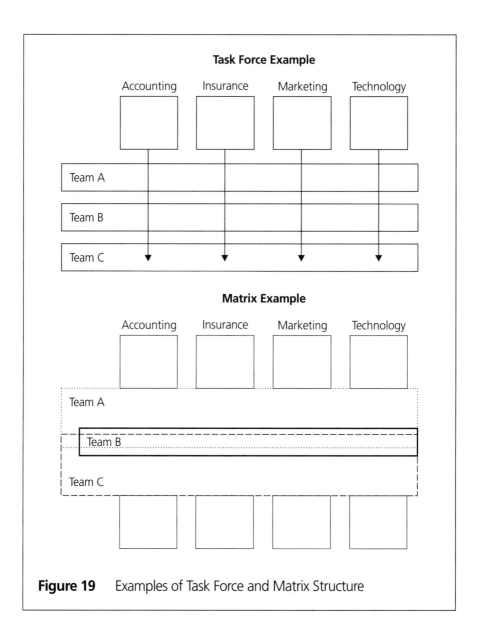

Figure 19 Examples of Task Force and Matrix Structure

Tools and Tips for Today's Project Manager

MEAN

The mean, also called the average, is the sum of all observations divided by the total number of observations. The common formula for the mean is:

$$\overline{X} = \Sigma x/n$$

The Σ (sigma) symbol represents *the summation of* the x observations; n, the total number of observations; and $\overline{X}$, the mean.

The mean is easy to calculate. It does not require preparing data before calculating it, but it does have its downside. If the number of observations is small, the dispersion between the lowest and highest values can skew the results of the calculation.

 for Calculating the Mean

- Determine the number of observations.
- Take the observations.
- Sum the observations.
- Divide the sum of observations by the number of observations to derive the average.

Median

The median is the midpoint average for a range of values. Fifty percent of the values are above the midpoint, and 50 percent are below it.

The following equations show the common formulas for the median.

- For an odd number of values:

    median = the middle value.

- For an even number of values:

    median = (summed values of the two middle values) / 2.

The benefits of the median are that it is easy to calculate. It is also not affected by extreme values. However, the downside is that it requires preparing the data before calculating it.

 for Calculating the Median

- Determine the number of observations.
- Take the observations.
- Sort the data.
- Determine whether an odd or even number of observations exist.
- If an odd number, pick the middle value.
- If an even number, pick the two middle values, add them together, and divide the sum by two to get the median.

Meetings

Have you ever attended a meeting where sharp disagreements were the norm rather than the exception? Where everyone concentrated on one topic at the expense of others? Where a few people dominated while the rest remained silent? Where decisions were the result of conformity (often called the move-toward-control tendency) rather than intelligent discussion? Where decisions were rushed, leaving little time for discussion? Where everyone strayed from the main issue?

The answer to one or more of the above questions is probably yes. Why? Because meetings are often poorly planned, organized, controlled, and led. Meetings, of course, do not have to be that way.

Running an effective meeting requires advance preparation. It also requires that the focus remain in sight at all times during the meeting. For a meeting to be meaningful, everyone should feel that a need or want was satisfied in the end.

The benefits of an effective meeting are many. It distributes information to wide numbers of people and provides the opportunity to resolve issues. It also encourages interaction and, consequently, *teaming*, while enabling sharing of experiences and knowledge that would ordinarily not occur.

 for Conducting Effective Meetings

- Determine the goal of the meeting.
- List the attendees.
- Prepare an agenda.
- Set the time and location.
- Identify all equipment and supply requirements.
- Facilitate, don't dominate, the meeting.
- Solicit everyone's input.
- Pace the meeting according to the agenda.
- Identify any remaining issues, whether listed or not listed on the agenda.
- Document the results of the meeting (e.g., in the form of minutes).

MEMO OF UNDERSTANDING

A memo of understanding records any agreements made during a meeting. It is sent to all attendees and other parties, like senior managers, who must keep informed of the results. It states the objectives of the meeting as well as when and where it occurred. It also identifies who agreed to what.

Several advantages accrue from a memo of understanding. First, it cements agreements and reduces misunderstandings. Second, it serves as a historical record of the agreements made. Third, it serves as a source document for subsequent actions. Finally, it reduces finger pointing since it reduces the opportunity for people to accuse others of not abiding by their agreements.

 for Developing a Memo of Understanding

- Date the memo.
- Identify all the addresses, including direct recipients and those receiving courtesy copies.
- Identify the subject in a few simple words. In the text, record the most important information first, followed by the least important.
- Sign the memo along with your phone number, mailstop, and E-mail address so that others can contact you.

METHODOLOGY DEVELOPMENT

A methodology is a formalized approach for managing or executing a process or project. It includes tasks, responsibilities, deliverables, and evaluation criteria.

A good methodology has several characteristics. It is documented, and it presents a road map that is easy to follow. It is also definitive but flexible enough to use in responding to different situations, and it provides illustrations of inputs and outputs.

A methodology offers several benefits. It provides guidance in handling ambiguous situations, provides discipline in managing or executing a process or project, and improves productivity. It also generates confidence and provides a common standard for operating.

 for Methodology Development

- Obtain input from the users of the methodology.
- Document the methodology.
- Define inputs and deliverables.
- Provide a sequence of tasks to implement the entire methodology.
- Define all terms.
- Distribute or provide access to the methodology.
- Use plenty of illustrations and examples.
- Keep it current and easy to use.

METRICS

Metrics are measures used to establish standards and track progress against those standards. Metrics and quality are often associated together; however, metrics can be used for establishing and tracking performance with respect to cost, schedule, people, and many other areas of interest.

Good metrics have certain characteristics. They are based upon expected versus actuals and upon some objective criteria. They are also applied consistently to determine trends and to identify and analyze variances to expected results.

The benefits of metrics are threefold. They help to track and monitor performance. They also help to identify areas for process improvement. Finally, they provide an audit trail to determine the cause of anomalies.

 for Establishing and Using Metrics

- Define the purpose of a metric.
- Determine its algorithm.
- Define its audience.
- Establish a means for collecting data.
- Determine where to get the data.
- Document the process or subject being measured.
- Determine the standard to measure against.
- Determine how to display the results of the measure (e.g., graph, chart).

MIND MAPPING

Mind mapping is a technique that enables you to *brainstorm*, that is, to let your thoughts flow freely. It works by allowing spontaneous thoughts on a particular topic to flow unchecked, then recording them on paper. While writing each thought, you draw a circle or bubble around each one and connect it with a related idea. Remember, each bubble represents a thought, and each thought is connected to a related one.

When mind mapping, do not evaluate an idea until you've completed the entire diagram. If you judge too early, you will consciously and subconsciously filter ideas.

After completing mind mapping, you must bring order to your creation. Go through the diagram and eliminate, add, or modify ideas. Then create some sort of sketch, memo, or report by referring to the diagram.

Mind mapping is advantageous because it is easy and can be fun to do. It also enables the identification of relationships among ideas.

 for Mind Mapping

- Clear your mind of all preconceived notions.
- On a piece of paper or using computer software, draw a circle. Inside it, write your main thought.
- Start drawing circles, writing the applicable thought inside each one.
    - Note: Related thoughts should be close to each other.
- As you draw circles, be sure to draw a line connecting all the related thoughts, which will show their relationships.

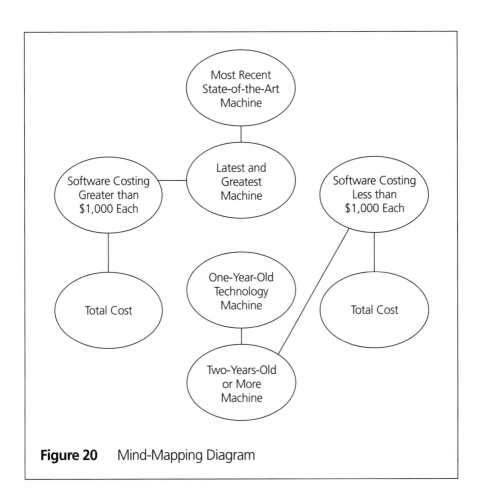

Figure 20   Mind-Mapping Diagram

MINUTES

One of the greatest fears people have is committing themselves to what they have said or promised to do and then not following through. No finer example exists than what occurs in a committee meeting, but minutes are a way to ensure follow-through.

Minutes can be useful if they have certain characteristics. They should contain sufficient detail about who said what and should be reviewed prior to publication. They also should be distributed to everyone who participated in the meeting.

The advantages of minutes are threefold. One, they capture who said what, thereby providing an audit trail. Two, they provide information for decision-making. Three, they reduce the learning curve for people new to an organization or project.

 for Taking Minutes

- Determine the level of detail for the minutes.
- Identify on the minutes the date, time, location, and the purpose of the meeting.
- Type the minutes.
- Attach copies of the minutes and supporting documentation.
- Distribute for comments or review at the next meeting.
- Incorporate revisions.
- Publish the minutes.

MODE

The mode is the most common value that appears in a distribution. The formula for calculating the mode is to count the value that appears the most frequently.

The benefits of the mode are that it is easy to calculate and does not require preparing the data if the number of values is small. The downside occurs if there are two or more modal values.

 for Calculating the Mode

- Determine the number of observations.
- Take the observations.
- If the number of observations is large, sort them.
- Count the value that appears the most frequently.

5, 7, 9, 1, 2, 4, 6, 8, 7, 3	1, 2, 3, 4, 5, 6, 7, 7, 8, 9
Unsorted List of Numbers	Sorted List of Numbers with 7 as the Mode

Figure 21   Example of Calculating Mode

MODELING

Modeling is using a physical or graphical representation to explain how a process or object works.

A good model has certain characteristics. It simplifies understanding, provides clarity, and maintains consistent symbology.

A wide range of models exists. Some are mathematical, such as Monte Carlo simulations. Some are graphical like data flow diagrams and flow charts. Whether mathematical or graphical, people who use them must first learn how to interpret them and see the value for their use.

A model provides three advantages. One, it communicates more clearly than narrative text. Two, it is a compact way to display information; three, it can be used to demonstrate ideas.

 for Modeling

- Determine the purpose of the model.
- Develop a standardized set of symbols with respective definitions.
- When drawing the model, keep it clear, simple, and consistent.
- Include a legend and title.
- Test the model prior to releasing it to the public.
- Obtain feedback and improve the model over time.

MYERS-BRIGGS TYPE INDICATOR

The Myers-Briggs Type Indicator is a psychological tool for determining personality preferences. There are sixteen personality types predicated upon the confirmation of four preferences. The four preferences are extroversion versus introversion, intuition versus sensation, thinking versus feeling, and judging versus perceiving. The resulting sixteen personality types manifest themselves through relationships, attitudes, viewpoints, interests, and so forth.

One benefit of the Myers-Briggs Type Indicator is that it is based on reliable research. Another benefit is that it has widespread acceptance. The challenges of the indicator are that it requires considerable training, and therefore, is not easily applied to real-life situations.

 for Using the Myers-Briggs Type Indicator

- Understand the four preferences.
- Observe the attitudes, relationships, viewpoints, and so on, of people.
- Determine the personality type.
- Match tasks to perform with the personality type.

NEGOTIATIONS

A common misperception is that negotiation is a *winner-take-all* endeavor. Hence, it's not surprising that so many negotiations end in a stalemate. In reality, the most desirable outcome of a negotiation is a win-win result in which everyone feels good about the agreement.

Effective negotiations share some other common characteristics besides having a win-win result. The negotiators have a strategy, and the negotiating team is unified. The team also knows as much as possible about the opposition, including their goals and objectives.

Effective negotiation offers many benefits. It encourages communication and teaming. It also furthers understanding and gives new insights and ideas. Finally, it provides the groundwork for taking action.

 ## for Conducting Effective Negotiations

- Determine your goals and objectives.
- Determine a strategy for achieving goals and objectives.
- Ensure that the negotiation team is united and behind the goals, objectives, and strategy.
- Select one person as the primary negotiator.
- Be flexible instead of *fluid*.
- Know as much as possible about the opposition.
- Know when to *push* and when to *yield*.
- Seek a win-win result.

NET PRESENT VALUE

Net present value (NPV) is a method for selecting an alternative that offers the best investment. It accounts for the time value of money, as well as identifies which alternative provides a rate of return greater than that provided by a financial institution. If the resulting calculation is greater than that earned at a bank, then it is okay to make the investment.

The advantages of NPV are twofold. It provides the financial basis for deciding whether to make an investment. It also is a widely accepted method for making financial investments.

 for Calculating the Net Present Value

- Calculate the cost of a proposal.
- Calculate its savings.
- Determine the interest rate.
- Determine the number of years that savings will occur (e.g., three-to-five years).
- Use the following formula for each proposal on computer software:

$$\text{Net Present Value} = \frac{\text{Savings}_{\text{year 1}}}{(1 + \text{Interest Rate})} + \frac{\text{Savings}_{\text{year 2}}}{(1 + \text{Interest Rate})}$$

$$+ \frac{\text{Savings}_{\text{year 3}}}{(1 + \text{Interest Rate})} - \text{Cost of Proposal}$$

- Example: The savings for any given year is $1,000; the interest rate is 5 percent (or .05). The cost of the proposal is $2,000. Calculate the net present value.

$$\text{Net Present Value} = \frac{1,000}{(1 + .05)} + \frac{1,000}{(1 + .05)} + \frac{1,000}{(1 + .05)} - 2,000 = \$723.24$$

- Note: A positive value suggests investing in the proposal. A negative value suggests investing it in a different place of higher return.

NETWORK DIAGRAM

A network diagram is a schedule to follow during a project. It consists of tasks arranged logically with each one having a start and finish date.

The network diagram presents a wealth of information to help you manage your project. It shows the tasks to complete, when to complete them, and in what sequence.

It also gives you the critical path containing those tasks and tells you which tasks need top priority and must be addressed without delay. You can identify the critical path because it is the longest path through the network diagram. You can calculate it by adding the durations of activities on each path; the path with the largest sum is your critical path.

The advantages of a network diagram are twofold: you can use it to manage the details of your project, and you can use it to communicate with your project team. However, avoid using it to communicate with senior management, who want only summary information.

 for Developing a Network Diagram

- Identify the tasks to perform.
- Logically connect the tasks together to reflect the desired sequence for performing them.
- Determine the flow time for each task.
- Using the logic and the duration of each task, calculate the start and finish dates.
    - Note: To calculate the start and finish dates, move from left to right in the network diagram.

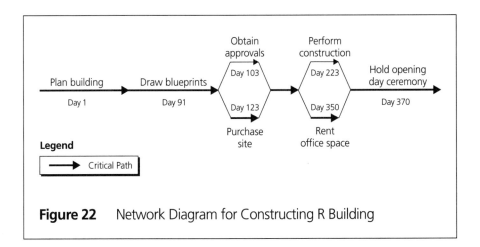

Figure 22   Network Diagram for Constructing R Building

Newsletter

A newsletter is a communications medium. It can cover a wide spectrum of topics. Policies, procedures, technology, and business issues are just some categories of topics to cover in the newsletter.

Your newsletter doesn't need a *Madison Avenue look*. With the power of desktop publishing offering WYSIWYG (what you see is what you get) capabilities, you can create a relatively professional-looking document containing graphics as well as text. Within minutes, you can produce a master document that's ready for reproduction on a copier—no need to mess with typeset or ink.

The best time to prepare a newsletter is when you're working on a project that requires visibility and the support of many people. The newsletter can help you keep them current on what has been and will be happening. Generally, the larger the number of people affected by a project, the greater the need for a newsletter.

A newsletter offers many benefits. It serves as reference material for new and existing employees. It also serves as a communications tool for employees wanting to learn the latest about a topic.

 for Developing a Newsletter

- Identify the purpose of the newsletter.
- Identify topics that will help achieve the purpose.
- Assign writers to the topics.
- Determine the layout, including graphics.
- Prepare the article(s).
- Reproduce the newsletter, either electronically or in hardcopy.

No!

"No!" is a two-letter word that most of us learned to say at two or three years old. As we grew older, for some strange reason, we found it difficult to use the word; instead, adults reply with a three-letter word—"Yes!"—even when we really want to say no.

Hence, this reluctance to say no is the reason for the demise of careers for many professionals. They have been asked to do something that may be unsuitable to their skills, experience, and availability. They said yes when they really wanted to say no just to keep peace with colleagues and superiors. The long-term result only angers colleagues and superiors who will discover your inability to deliver at some future date.

If you're like many people, you hate to say no. The urge for acceptance overwhelms the need for setting priorities and not worrying about what other people think. Here are some key points to help you learn to say no.

What matters is not saying no, but how you say it. Sometimes you can say no by never saying it. For instance, you can tell the person asking you to do something that you will address her need after you complete a long list of items. (Do not say that they are higher priority.) You are then sending a subtle message that the person must wait, which she may not be willing to do and, therefore, will go someplace else.

Saying no offers several advantages. It avoids overcommitting yourself and keeps you from putting yourself in a situation that you do not want to be in. Finally, it builds self-confidence and self-respect.

 TNT for Saying No!

- Keep your main goal(s) in the forefront of your mind.
- Listen to the request, and evaluate it from the perspective of your main goal(s).
- Try to understand the reason for the request. If it fails to further your goal(s), give it a priority relative to yours.
- Muster the courage to say no, accompanied with an explanation.
- If you are given more than one request of equal priority, ask the requester to determine which is more important.

NONMONETARY REWARDS

Most people believe rewards come only in monetary forms. In reality, you can reward people for doing something without offering money, even if you have no formal authority. You can give nonmonetary rewards that cost you only time and a little effort.

The idea of nonmonetary rewards is not new but is often overlooked in the business world. Frederick Herzberg and Abraham Maslow, both management specialists, have developed useful theories on the topic. Perhaps the greatest practitioner of the nonmonetary reward is the military; it continually offers people nonmonetary rewards.

Several nonmonetary rewards exist, such as praising people to their boss, writing a letter of appreciation and sending it to their management, and sending a thank you card. You can also take people to lunch or even dinner, or you can give them tickets to a social event. You may simply give them a pat on the shoulder or a handshake. Any of these rewards are appreciable for a job well done.

The positive side for rewarding people for their help is that it serves as an investment. The next time you need their help, they'll remember the reward and will continue the fine support.

 for Determining Nonmonetary Rewards

- Identify the principal values of the organization.
- Understand the history behind the types of awards given.
- Develop objective criteria for determining who should receive what reward.
- Maintain objectivity in administering the evaluation criteria.
- Determine the frequency and overall value of the reward.

OBJECT VERSUS PROCESS ANALYSIS

Increasingly, object analysis is becoming the preferred mode of modeling vis-à-vis process analysis. The fundamental difference between the two is that object analysis relies on the relationships among entities (e.g., people, organizations) while process analysis relies on the exchange of data among processes.

Both object and process analysis have their origins in the information technology arena. Some popular object analysis approaches include ones by Coad and Yourdon, Jones, Booch, and Rumbaugh. Some popular process analysis approaches include ones by DeMarco, Gane and Sarson, and Hatley and Pirbhai.

Object analysis is becoming more popular with the advent of client/server computing, object-event programming, and reengineering. Its advantages are its reflection of real-world objects and their relationships and its translation to more contemporary business practices (e.g., reengineering). Process analysis, although widely used, is associated more with mainframe environments and process-oriented environments. Its advantages are its ease of application, history of application, and limited number of varieties.

 for Using Object versus Process Analysis

- Determine the purpose of the analysis (e.g., use for object-oriented programming).
- Determine which type of analysis is more familiar to people (e.g., clients, analysts).
- Determine whether flow of control is an issue.
  - Note: Object analysis handles flow of control better than data flows.
- Whether object analysis or process analysis, understand:
  - the notation
  - overall architecture
  - desired characteristics of models.

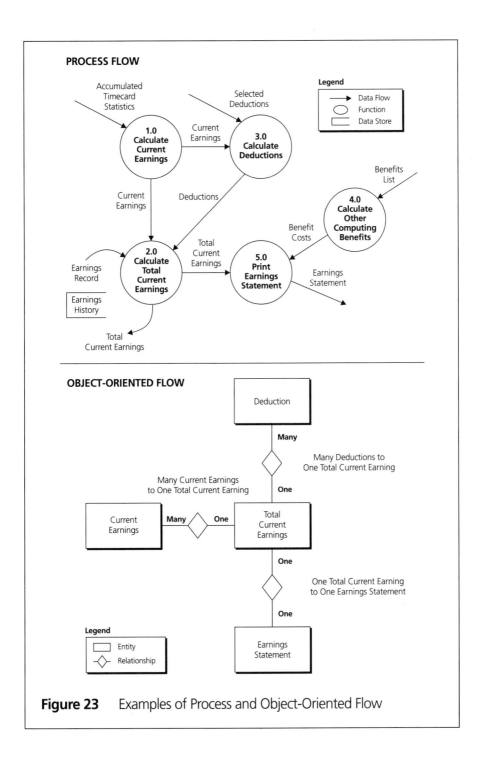

PROCESS FLOW

Accumulated Timecard Statistics

Selected Deductions

Legend
- → Data Flow
- ○ Function
- ▭ Data Store

1.0 Calculate Current Earnings

Current Earnings

3.0 Calculate Deductions

Current Earnings

Deductions

4.0 Calculate Other Computing Benefits

Benefits List

Benefit Costs

Earnings Record

2.0 Calculate Total Current Earnings

Total Current Earnings

5.0 Print Earnings Statement

Earnings Statement

Earnings History

Total Current Earnings

OBJECT-ORIENTED FLOW

Deduction

Many

Many Deductions to One Total Current Earning

One

Many Current Earnings to One Total Current Earning

Current Earnings

Many — One

Total Current Earnings

One

One Total Current Earning to One Earnings Statement

One

Legend
- ▭ Entity
- ◇ Relationship

Earnings Statement

Figure 23   Examples of Process and Object-Oriented Flow

OPERATIONS MANUAL

An operations manual is a compilation of administrative documentation that people reference during their daily activities. An office, entire organization, or a project can have an operations manual.

What goes in an operations manual? Plenty. You can have copies of forms and instructions for completing them; copies of procedures on personnel, logistical, transportation, and other administrative matters; phone and equipment lists; organization charts; and anything else you deem important.

Your operations manual need not look like the product of a giant publishing house. You can place the material in a three-ring binder. You can also group the contents according to some logical schema and separate each group by a divider.

The operations manual is advantageous because it is a communications medium that provides standards and guidelines for doing business.

 for Developing an Operations Manual

- Determine the scope of the manual.
- Determine the contents of the manual (e.g., forms, personnel, equipment, organization).
- Prepare a table of contents.
- Assign someone to initially develop and eventually maintain the manual.
- Determine the mode of distribution (e.g., hardcopy, Web).
- Determine the binding, if applicable.

I. **Introduction**
   A. Preface
   B. Table of Contents
   C. Table of Illustrations

II. **Overviews**
   A. Vision
   B. Background and History
   C. Organization

III. **Administrative**
   A. Personnel
   B. Policies
   C. Procedures

IV. **Appendices**

V. **Index**

Figure 24   Sample Outline of an Operations Manual

ORGANIZATION CHART

The organization chart graphically shows reporting relationships using a series of boxes and lines. The boxes represent positions and lines that reflect the reporting relationships.

You can draw an organization structure based upon function, region, product, or a combination thereof. Whichever one you choose, however, the organization chart should seek to achieve several objectives.

First, it should streamline operations. The chart should reflect minimum layers to meet managerial needs. Too many layers produces waste and breeds inefficiency.

Second, it should maximize resource usage. No chart should contain positions that contribute little or nothing toward achieving an organization's goals and objectives.

Third, it should improve communication and reporting relationships. No chart should contain a structure that obscures reporting relationships by having, for instance, a position reporting to more than one supervisor.

Fourth, it should reflect an optimum level of responsibility and accountability. For instance, a supervisory position should have no more than ten people reporting to it and not less than five. Too many reflects a span of control that is too wide, and too few reflects a span of control that is too narrow.

Fifth, it should contribute to attaining organizational goals and objectives. If you can't explain how your organization chart will help contribute to meeting organizational goals and objectives, then change it. If the chart leads your organization in a different direction, you'll have performance problems.

An organization chart offers several benefits. It clarifies reporting relationships and identifies responsibilities. It also clarifies communications and enables structuring in a manner that increases effectiveness.

for Developing an Organization Chart

- Identify the functional and process units.
- Identify the reporting relationships within each functional and process unit.
- Maintain effective spans of control with each functional and process unit.
- Ensure that, overall, the entire organization has clear reporting relationships and effective spans of control.

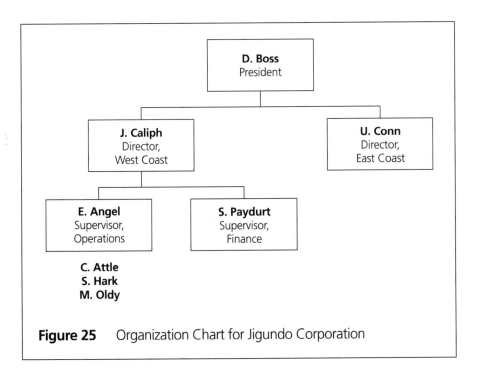

Figure 25 Organization Chart for Jigundo Corporation

ORGANIZING

Organizing is setting up an infrastructure to manage a project effectively and efficiently. The infrastructure includes assigning responsibilities, defining reporting relationships, and developing documentation media (e.g., forms, reports).

Some specific actions for organizing a company or project include:

- developing and publishing an organization chart
- establishing regular communications (e.g., staff meetings)
- setting up information centers
- developing and publishing forms and reports.

Organizing not only applies resources efficiently and effectively, but also focuses on the major issues of a project. Finally, a well-organized project can largely *run on its own*.

 for Organizing

- Determine the goals of a project.
- Conduct an inventory of resources available to the project.
- Assign resources in a manner that best achieves the goals.
- Determine the communications requirements for conducting the project.
- Develop media (e.g., reports) and approaches (e.g., meetings) for capturing or dispensing information, keeping in mind the audience (e.g., senior management).
- Determine processes for executing the project.
- Document the processes.

OUTLINE

Many people go through agony when writing even the first sentence of a memo or report. The experience is so intense, in fact, that they close the door to their office and copy the work of someone else or take their work home and have their spouse complete the first draft. Yet they could have avoided such humiliation by drafting an outline before writing the first sentence.

All documents have the same three-part structure, and outlines mimic it. The three parts are the introduction, discussion, and conclusion.

The introduction provides an overview of the topic. It covers the scope, goals, and objectives of the subject. This part typically consumes 10 percent of the outline.

The discussion covers the major topics and their subtopics. You can organize topics and subtopics sequentially, chronologically, spatially, or through a mixture of the three. This part typically consumes 80 percent of the outline.

The conclusion summarizes the highlights covered in the discussion, but it does *not* rehash the discussion point by point. This part consumes 10 percent of the outline.

Outlining offers several benefits. It not only forces you to organize your thoughts, but it also provides the structure for preparing a presentation or a narrative document. Finally, it provides a means for seeking input prior to preparing a draft.

 for Building an Outline

- Define the topic for the outline in one sentence.
- On a sheet of paper or using computer software, compose the words *introduction, discussion,* and *conclusion,* leaving sufficient room for the next step(s).
- Under the introduction, list the goals, scope, and objectives of the document.
- In the discussion, list the details for each topic that you identify.
- In the discussion, arrange each topic and the subtopics in logical order (e.g., spatially).
- In the conclusion, list the major points presented in the discussion.

OUTSOURCING

Outsourcing is having a third party provide services that would ordinarily be offered in-house. It can be used for just about any function or process. The only question is whether it is cost-effective vis-à-vis the same function or service in-house.

Outsourcing offers three benefits. One, it can save money. Two, it can provide better quality of service, and three, it can provide flexibility. However, outsourcing can boomerang in three ways: it can cost more in the long run, can cause dependency on third parties, and can demoralize the workforce.

 ## for Deciding Whether to Outsource

- Define requirements for functions and/or processes.
- Select from a list of outsourcing vendors.
- Identify critical and noncritical functions and processes.
- Perform cost-benefit and value analysis under different scenarios.
- Investigate the history of each outsourcing vendor.
- Determine each vendor's capability to provide the desired level of service.
- Include a contract service-level agreement, replete with rewards and penalties.

Overcoming Bottlenecks

A bottleneck is a snag in the business process, or a way of doing business, that causes work to pile up. When work piles up, little progress occurs because the bottleneck acts as a traffic jam, preventing any further movement forward. So what do you do?

You analyze the problem and determine the cause of the bottleneck. A good way to do this is to view the bottleneck as a car on a highway that stalls and blocks the autos behind it. You should fix the cause of the traffic jam, but the tendency is to go around the stalled car rather than fix it, which may get the traffic moving again but will not eliminate the cause of the jam. Sooner or later the traffic jam will occur again, perhaps at a less opportune time, such as when the volume of traffic increases.

The benefits of overcoming bottlenecks are obvious. It enables productivity to *hum*, thereby increasing efficiency and effectiveness. It also increases morale by removing opportunities for frustration to arise. Further, it shortens the time of delivery to the customer and reduces the need for inventory.

 for Overcoming Bottlenecks

- Develop a flowchart of the *as-is* process as it occurs with the bottleneck.
- Identify the who, what, when, where, why, and how for each step in the flowchart.
- Identify points that increase cycle time, such as too many review and approval cycles.
- Develop a flow chart of the *to-be* process that will eliminate the bottleneck.

P²M² Cycle

The P²M² (practical project management methodology) cycle is the decision-making model for use in a project environment. It consists of five elements: inputs, tasks, responsibilities, outputs, and measures of success.

Inputs feed specific tasks. People have specific responsibilities for performing those tasks in order to create specific outputs. The outputs meet specific criteria, called measures of success.

A major advantage of the cycle is that it is a simple model to follow. It also provides a model that leads to improved performance because it spirals and is iterative.

 for Applying the P²M² Cycle

- Determine goals of the project.
- Determine the tasks to accomplish the goals.
- For each task, determine the inputs, responsibilities, and outputs.
- For each output, determine the measures of success, or quality criteria.

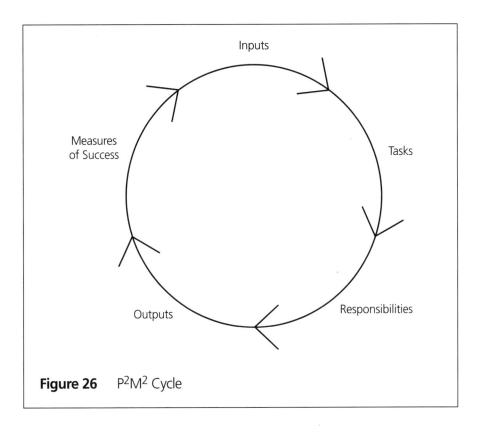

Figure 26   P²M² Cycle

PARADIGMS

A paradigm is a model, complete with values and beliefs, that is used to perceive reality. In other words, it provides an all-encompassing way to interpret and interact with the world.

A paradigm can last a long time, as long as it works. Sometimes, a *crack* in the paradigm lays the groundwork for a new one with its own values and beliefs. Almost immediately the new paradigm replaces the old one.

The advantages of paradigms are that they provide order, predictability, consistency, and reliability. The downside is that they can lead to rigidity, resistance to change, and bias. It is important to be able to manage the impact of paradigms, especially when multiple paradigms exist.

 for Dealing with Paradigms

- Define the goals and objectives to achieve.
- Identify the values and beliefs that will support the achievement of the goals and objectives.
- Identify the values and beliefs that will resist the achievement of goals and objectives.
- Identify which people and organizations contain the values and beliefs that will further achieve the goals and objectives.
- Identify which people and organizations harbor the values and beliefs that lead to resistance to achieving the goals and objectives.
- Develop a plan for capitalizing on the values and beliefs that support achieving the goals and objectives and overcoming resistance.
- Execute the plan.

PARETO ANALYSIS

The idea that a few can determine an outcome is known as the Pareto analysis rule. This rule assumes that 80 percent of the effects are attributed to 20 percent of the causes. The Pareto chart illustrates the causes of effects.

The Pareto chart is a bar chart that highlights and differentiates the major cause from the minor causes. With the chart, you can address those causes with the highest frequency of occurrences instead of those with low frequency. In other words, you can dedicate time, resources, and effort to the most important causes, not the least important ones.

The Pareto analysis rule makes sense, as it did in the early part of this century when the great Italian economist Vilfredo Pareto developed the idea while studying crime and wealth concentration. Over eighty years later, the Pareto analysis rule has even greater relevance in other environments.

Pareto analysis offers several benefits. It helps to distinguish the actual causes and helps differentiate between what is and is not important. It is also easy to perform after the compilation of data.

 for Performing Pareto Analysis

- Compile and sort the data according to some predetermined criteria.
- Draw an x-axis (horizontal line).
- Segment the line into parts for each type of criterion.
- Draw a y-axis (vertical line).
- Graduate the y-axis to reflect the cumulative frequency of occurrence (e.g., total number).
- Draw a vertical bar to reflect the cumulative frequency for each type of problem.
    - Note: For readability, draw the bars in descending order—that is, draw the bar with the highest frequency of occurrence first, then down to the least.

Frequency	Description
15	Not Enough Money
10	Not Enough Time
8	Not Enough Storage

Figure 27   Pareto Analysis for Little Theatre Wardrobe Department

Tools and Tips for Today's Project Manager

PARKINSON'S LAW

In today's business environment, business professionals and managers allude to Parkinson's Law. It states that work expands to fill the time available for its completion. If you have ten hours available to do a job, for example, you'll take the full ten hours to complete it. The basis for this law is that people will fill the vacuum created by the time assigned to perform a task, even if it means procrastinating.

For most tasks, Parkinson's Law makes sense. Having too much time to complete a task leads to statusing games like the 90 percent syndrome. This syndrome occurs when people say they're 90 percent done with a task, until, at the last minute, they slide the final completion date. The question then arises: whatever happened to the last 10 percent?

Understanding Parkinson's Law provides several benefits for project assignment. It enables you to reevaluate time estimates, and it gives you clues into what tasks to monitor more closely than others. It also encourages maintaining a healthy skepticism when status information is submitted.

 for Overcoming Parkinson's Law

- Determine priorities.
- Give more time to top priorities.
- Use reliable estimating techniques.
- Take frequent measurements on performance.
- Maintain visibility of those measurements.

Participative Decision-Making

A misconception exists in the business world that participative decision-making means that everyone makes the decision. What participative management really involves is one or more individuals receiving input from all pertinent individuals prior to making a decision.

Also, contrary to popular belief, participative management does not absolve the decision-makers from responsibility or accountability. For some reason, many people believe that receiving input from other people dilutes the responsibility or accountability for the decision. The responsibility and accountability for a decision still rests with the decision-maker.

Whatever your position within an organization, you'll likely use participative decision-making. Here are three tips to remember when using this method.

One, use participative decision-making when your decision affects several critical people who are not within your chain of command. Failure to solicit input from those people makes implementing your decision difficult because you lack command and control over them.

Two, provide sufficient time to solicit input from everyone. Avoid setting a rigid deadline unless circumstances demand it. You want quality input, but setting an unrealistic deadline can mean little or no input.

Three, remain objective. Receive input whether or not you agree with it. The idea is to receive all input so you can make the best possible decision. If you become evaluative before making a decision, the likelihood of a flawed decision increases.

Participating decision-making offers several advantages. It builds commitment, eases implementation of a decision, and lowers the potential for resistance. It also encourages involvement from people who can affect the outcome of a decision.

for Encouraging Greater Participative Decision-Making

■ Seek input prior to making a decision.
■ Take the initiative in obtaining input.
■ Provide opportunities for input (e.g., frequent staff meetings, one-on-one sessions).
■ Conduct follow-up with participants after making the decision.

PAYBACK ANALYSIS

Payback analysis is simply determining the number of years that it takes for a new product, service, and so forth, to accumulate earnings to pay for itself.

There are, of course, a number of variables that affect the payback period of a new product or service. These include taxes, fees, and so on, and should be accounted for when determining the payback period.

The benefit of payback analysis is determining which new variety of product or service offers the greatest return to offset investment and implementation costs. It also facilitates deciding whether to proceed.

 for Determining Payback Analysis

- Exactly define the new product, service, and so on.
- Calculate its cumulative cost.
- Perform a breakeven analysis.
- Determine the payback period by using the following formula:

$$\frac{\text{Investment}}{\text{Average Year Return on Investment}}$$

- For each alternative for a new product, service, and so on, calculate the expected annual rate of return.
- Draw a matrix to reflect the varying rates of return for each alternative.
  - Note: Decide whether to deduct taxes, fees, and so on, prior to calculation.
- Select the alternative that offers the most desirable rate of return.

	Alternative ($ in thousands)		
Year	A	B	C
1	100	60	50
2	50	60	50
3	50	60	50
4	50	60	50
5	50	60	100
Total Return	**300**	**300**	**300**

Table 12   Payback Period for Machine Shop Y

PERT Estimating Technique

Determining the time needed to complete a task is difficult. An unlimited number of variables are involved, making it impossible to completely account for them. The best approach is to develop an estimate that you have a high level of confidence in reaching. The PERT (program evaluation review technique) estimating technique can help you do that.

The PERT estimating technique involves the use of three variables for calculating the overall time to complete a task. The three variables are the most optimistic, most pessimistic, and most likely times.

The most optimistic (mo) estimate is the time needed to complete a task under the *best* conditions. The most pessimistic (mp) estimate is the time needed to complete a task under the *worst* conditions. The most likely (ml) estimate is the time needed to complete a task under *normal* conditions.

The PERT estimating technique offers several benefits. One, it gives more reliable estimates. Two, it is easy to calculate, although it is time consuming. Three, it is superior to other estimating techniques.

The variables are used for the expected time. The expected time is then adjusted to account for nonproductive time (e.g., time for going to the restroom, chatting about nonwork-related topics).

TNT for Using the PERT Estimating Technique

- Develop a complete work breakdown structure.
- For each task, determine most pessimistic, most likely, and most optimistic times.
  - Note: Do this for only the lowest levels of the work breakdown structure.
- Calculate the expected time for each task.

$$\text{Estimate}_{time} = \frac{mo + 4\,(ml) + mp}{6}$$

  - Example: Most optimistic time is ten, most likely is twenty, and most pessimistic is thirty.

$$\text{Example}_{time} = \frac{10 + 4\,(20) + 30 = 20}{6}$$

- Estimate the percent of nonproductive time.
- Calculate the adjusted expected time for each task.

Adjusted Expected$_{time}$ = (Nonproductive Time) x (Expected$_{time}$)

  - Example: Nonproductive time is 10 percent (or 100 percent plus 10 percent, which equals 110 percent or 1.10).

Adjusted Expected$_{time}$ = 1.10 x 20 = 22 Hours Adjusted Expected$_{time}$

PETER PRINCIPLE

Lawrence J. Peter introduced a principle that struck a universal chord when he published the Peter Principle. The Peter Principle was simple and relevant to everyone working in a bureaucracy. It said that in a hierarchy, every individual rises to a level of incompetence and advances no further. It applied to both public and private institutions.

Keeping the Peter Principle in mind, you'll recognize that a person who has reached a level of incompetence often becomes an obstacle to greater performance or change. Hence, a corollary to the Peter Principle exists: a person who reaches a level of incompetence is an obstacle to progress. They're like *brick walls* that won't let anything pass. These people are often negative, even hostile, because they do not want anyone to surpass them or upset their position, which would only reinforce their feelings of incompetence and may threaten their position.

Understanding the Peter Principle offers two benefits. It helps you in identifying who will embrace your idea, technique, and so forth, and who will not. It will also help you in developing an effective strategy for bypassing the brick wall.

 for Dealing with People Who Have Made the Peter Principle a Reality

- Recognize that the person is a manifestation of the principle.
- Go around the individual; do not bother dealing with that person directly.
- Make your case with facts and data, even when communicating with that person.

PHASE BREAKDOWN

If your projects are like most, they have five phases: feasibility, requirements, design, build, and implementation.

In the *feasibility phase*, you investigate whether your project is possible and acquire enough preliminary information on whether to continue the project. In the *requirements phase*, you acquire as much information as possible to complete your project and try to determine what you must fulfill before completing your project. In the *design phase*, you create a way to fulfill requirements and explore different approaches to meet those needs. In the *build phase*, you do something to meet the requirements and design, which involves constructing the output that you will deliver upon the project's completion. In the *implementation phase*, you place the output into the real world. No doubt, you will find the need to revise the output to increase its usefulness.

These phases can occur in several sequences. For example, they can occur linearly, such as feasibility, then requirements, and so on. Or some phases can occur in parallel, such as requirements and design phases occurring at the same time.

Breaking projects into phases offers many benefits. It simplifies the management of a project, allows for better planning, and increases understanding. It also helps to identify the relationships among the tasks and the different outputs created throughout the life cycle of a project.

 for Phase Breakdown

- Identify the product to build or the service to deliver.
- Identify the major *blocks* of activities or phases.
- Experiment with determining the sequence of those blocks.
- Select the sequence that best serves your needs.
- Identify the *demand* to produce, for each phase.

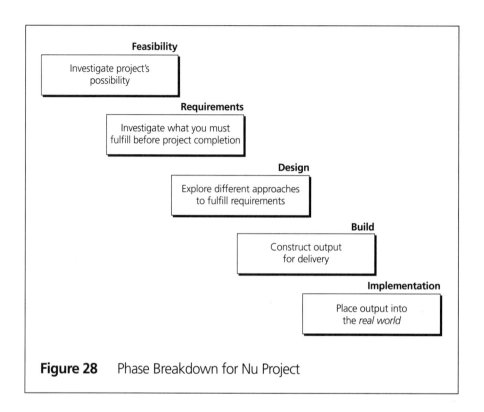

Figure 28   Phase Breakdown for Nu Project

PLANNING

Planning is determining in advance the goals to achieve and the path for achieving them. In other words, it answers what must be accomplished, how it must be done, and when it must be done.

Planning in an organization or for a project involves the following specific actions.

■ Determine the results to achieve.
■ Develop schedules and other road maps.
■ Allocate resources.
■ Estimate time and costs.

Planning offers many advantages. First, it enables more effective application of resources. Second, it allows for determining how well a project is accomplishing its goals. Third, it builds confidence in the people who must do the work, especially if they need a sense of direction and a defined path to follow.

 for Planning

■ Define the goals and objectives.
■ Develop a work breakdown structure.
■ Estimate hours needed to perform each task in the work breakdown structure.
■ Assign people to each task.
■ Develop a schedule.

POSDCORB

Just about any project involving two or more people requires POSDCORB, which stands for planning, organizing, staffing, directing, coordinating, reporting, and budgeting.

Planning entails deciding what tasks to perform, then determining their logical sequence and the time allotted to do them; *organizing*, defining organizational structure and responsibilities; *staffing*, acquiring people to fulfill organizational structures and responsibilities; *directing*, making decisions; *coordinating*, ensuring that all activities and events occur smoothly; *reporting*, obtaining useful feedback; and *budgeting*, designating or allocating monies to make the project happen. Failure to perform one or more of these tasks can seriously impair the progress of your project.

One benefit of POSDCORB is that it is easy to remember. Another is that it has been applied successfully in the past.

 for Implementing POSDCORB

- Identify all major planning activities.
- Identify all major organizing activities.
- Identify all staffing activities.
- Identify all directing activities.
- Identify all coordinating activities.
- Identify all reporting activities.
- Identify all budgetary activities.

PRESENTATIONS

While you may not have a gift for oratory, you can still give presentations that will enhance your career. However, effective presentations involve more than standing before people and talking. You also have the onus of getting them to listen to what you have to say and take action with it.

All presentations have three logical parts: introduction, body, and conclusion. The introduction presents the purpose of the presentation. The body presents the major points and the supporting details for each one, and the conclusion summarizes the main points in the body and ties back to the introduction.

The introduction and conclusion are key for communicating your points even though they comprise only a small portion of the presentation. In the introduction, you need to grab attention. In the conclusion, you need to inspire the audience to action.

Presentations, when designed and delivered well, offer several benefits. They communicate information clearly and concisely, and they motivate people. Finally, they provide an opportunity to further understand a topic.

 for Delivering Effective Presentations

- Avoid speaking more than fifty minutes without a break.
- Build a logical structure into your presentation (e.g., introduction, discussion, conclusion).
- Avoid distractive mannerisms.
- Be natural.
- Encourage questions from the audience.
- Use visible media (e.g., overhead transparencies, computer generated slides).
- Finish before the allotted time.
- Maintain eye contact with the audience.

PRIORITY SETTING

Setting priorities requires making hard decisions continually. It is troublesome because demands, requests, and tasks change constantly.

Despite the difficulty in making a decision about priorities, the process is simple: you categorize requests, demands, and tasks. For example, you might categorize them according to high, medium, and low priority.

High priority means addressing those items immediately; failure to do so will result in a *show stopper*. Medium priority means addressing those items after handling the high priority ones; failure to do so will not be an immediate show stopper but will become one later if left unattended. Low priority means addressing those items if time permits; failure to do so will not become a show stopper.

Categorizing is not an objective process. You must decide what goes into each category. Your decisions will depend on the nature of the demand, request, or task and on your experience. No mathematical calculation exists that will make your decisions easy.

Priority setting provides obvious advantages. It allows you to focus your energies and attention and enables you to address the most serious concerns first. It also makes effective use of time and other resources.

 for Priority Setting

- Determine your goal(s).
- As requests come in, evaluate them from the perspective of achieving the goal(s).
- Classify the goal(s) as high, medium, or low priority.
- Focus on the high priority request(s), noting a completion date and time.

Probability

Probability is determining the likelihood or *odds* that an event will occur. It is useful, therefore, for predicting outcomes of random trials. A subset of an outcome is an event, and it occurs when realized during a trial.

An occurrence of an event can happen when two or more events have no dependency on each other. Or an event can happen when two or more events are exclusive of each other. Regardless, the probability of an event can be calculated with or without prior observation. The sum of all probabilities must equal a value of one.

If no dependency exists between events, then the probability of their joint occurrences is the product of their individual probabilities. If a dependency exists, then the sum of their individual probabilities determines the probability of an occurrence of any event.

Probability calculations are useful for predicting outcomes. They are also useful for determining the accuracy of predictions.

 for Calculating Probabilities

- Determine the objective of the calculations.
- Determine whether probabilities should be calculated prior to or after trials.
- Determine if the events are independent or exclusive of each other.
- Determine the appropriate sample size.
- Determine the appropriate probability distribution to calculate (e.g., normal distribution, binomial distribution).
- Calculate the probabilities.
- Conduct tests to verify the accuracy of the predicted probabilities.

PROBLEM ANALYSIS AND SOLUTION

Whether at home, work, or on vacation, we all have problems. Wherever there are people, problems exist. Yet problems are not necessarily bad. They can become the springboard for new ideas, technological advancements, and better careers. The key is to handle a problem correctly.

Problem analysis requires that you first know a problem exists. It also demands the ability to divorce the symptoms from the causes. It then requires taking appropriate action, but only after identifying alternatives and testing. Yet problem analysis does not stop after implementation. It repeats itself continually to ensure the solution still works.

Problem analysis offers two benefits: it forces recognition that a problem exists and impels you to take action.

 for Problem Analysis and Solution

- Recognize that the problem exists.
- Define the problem.
- Identify the causes of the problem.
- Test the causes.
- Determine the solution.
- Implement the solution.
- Seek feedback.
- Take corrective action.

PROCEDURES

Relying on a few people for the information needed to perform a task makes little sense. These people may depart from the organization due to promotions, sickness, vacations, death, and so on. Yet few organizations record this information in procedures.

Procedures document how to perform tasks or conduct specific activities. They provide specific answers regarding who, what, when, where, why, and how.

Contrary to popular belief, preparing procedures on just about every conceivable topic is unnecessary and counterproductive. Procedures should only exist for topics concerning essential activities or atypical circumstances. The last thing you want are procedures that cover insignificant, minute details. You'll only waste time and money.

Well-written procedures share some common characteristics. They are brief, not exceeding more than a few pages. They also have plenty of white space; too much narrative text creates a mental block and makes searching for key information difficult. Furthermore, they give preference to pictures, charts, and diagrams, rather than narrative text to facilitate comprehension. Finally, they are clear and concise; that is, they do not look like an eighteenth-century novel.

Procedures offer several advantages. They reduce the effects of employee turnover or retirement as well as the learning curve for new staff. They also provide standards and guidelines for conducting business. Finally, they clearly define responsibilities and activities.

 for Developing Procedures

- Determine the topic.
- Define the scope and purpose.
- Define the audience.
- Develop an outline of the structure and contents.
- Draft the procedure.
- Edit for readability, information, and understanding.
- Verify the contents.
- Make revisions, if necessary.
- Publish the procedure.

PROCESS STREAMLINING

As an organization expands, it develops less-efficient organizational structures to conduct business. It can still achieve its goals and objectives, known as effectiveness, but does so wastefully. Streamlining is the process of identifying inefficient organizational structures and then making work proceed effectively, efficiently, and smoothly.

To streamline, you must recognize organizational waste when you see it. Some examples are: duplicate effort, unequal workload distribution, illogical task sequence, missed deadlines, poor workmanship, excessive delays, needless tasks, and positions having no productive value.

You have several methods available for identifying waste. You can review organization charts, prepare flowcharts, collect statistics, perform Pareto analysis, distribute questionnaires, and interview people. Using the information you acquire, you can then develop solutions that streamline your organization.

The benefits of process streamlining are obvious. It reduces waste and shortens the delivery cycle. It also increases output. Finally, it improves morale by lowering frustration.

 for Process Streamlining

- Encourage the people doing the work to participate.
- Document the existing process as a narrative or graphic.
- Identify areas of potential waste.
- Develop a more efficient and effective process.
- Perform a comparative analysis between the existing and proposed, or new, process.
- Communicate the results.

PROJECT ANNOUNCEMENT

The project announcement is a memo or bulletin that announces a project to a company's workforce. It can be in electronic or hardcopy form or both.

The benefits of a project announcement are twofold. It gives visibility to a project, and it shows management's support of the project, especially when signed by senior executives.

 for Creating a Project Announcement

- Identify the recipients of the announcement.
- Identify the *header* information (e.g., date, mail stops, subject).
- Determine the contents, including name and purpose of the project, the project manager, and schedule.
- Identify signatories of the announcement.

Date:

To:

Subject:

> *[Paragraph giving name and purpose of the project and name of the project manager]*

> *[Paragraph stating start and end dates of project plus any other relevant details]*

Signature / Date Block of Executive

Figure 29   Format of a Project Announcement

PROJECT LIFE CYCLE

Every project, to some extent, has its own unique characteristics, such as schedule and resource requirements. However, most projects progress through a life cycle consisting of several phases, though some projects may not progress through all the phases. In theory, a project that progresses from start to finish passes through five phases: conception, formulation, implementation, installation, and sustaining. The matrix in Table 13 shows each phase, including its definition and common output.

Knowing what phase of the life cycle a project is in offers three benefits. One, it indicates what may or may not have been done already. Two, it indicates how well the project is progressing. Three, it indicates what important issues the project may be facing.

 for Determining the Phase of a Project

- Review project documentation (e.g., reports, network diagrams) in the project history files.
- Review databases that feed automated scheduling software.
- Interview key participants for the project.
- Identify output to date and evaluate its completeness.

Phase	Definition	Output
Conception	Developing an Idea of What the Project Is to Build	Idea
Formulation	Developing a Plan for Realizing the Vision	Plan
Implementation	Executing the Plan	Components of a Product
Installation	Delivering the Product to the Client	Completed Product
Sustaining	Putting the Product in the Control of the Client	Operational Product

Table 13   Phases in a Project's Life Cycle

PROJECT OFFICE

A project office is a central place to lead, plan, organize, control, and close the activities of a project. It is also a place to obtain a *panoramic* view, that is, a view that avoids burying yourself in details.

A project office, therefore, is also an information center. It contains charts, diagrams, documentation, and schedules. It displays this information on walls, whiteboards, blackboards, and easel pads. Depending on your needs, it can even have audio-visual equipment. It houses the project team, too, especially individuals supporting the project on a full-time basis.

The benefits of a project office are threefold. One, it serves as a convenient communications hub. Two, it functions as a convenient meeting place. Three, it can serve as a central storage facility.

 for Establishing a Project Office

- Identify the goals of the project.
- Identify the supplies, equipment, information, and so on, required to monitor the performance of the project.
- Sketch the outlay of the office on paper or by using computer software.
- Set up the project office before the project begins.
- Keep the project office open.
- Keep it as the central communications hub throughout the life cycle of the project.

PROTOTYPE

You can build prototypes for many items, including sculptures, automobiles, airplanes, computing systems, buildings, homes, outhouses, and reports.

Building a prototype on a project makes good sense, particularly when the investment in time and money will be large. You will only be investing a fraction of money on a scaled down version of the final product. Hence, you save not only time and money but also gain effort and confidence.

What if you don't like the prototype? Then throw it away and build a new one. Imagine spending considerable money, time, and effort on something only to discover it's no good—and you must discard it! A prototype avoids that circumstance.

Prototyping has several benefits. It comes in different forms, and you can build a crude model of the final product that has little or no capabilities. You can also build a prototype that's just short of the final system. Or you can create a prototype that's simply a sketch on paper of the ultimate product.

 TNT for Developing a Prototype

- Define the requirements or specification.
- Develop the fundamental structure of the prototype.
- Verify the prototype to see if it satisfies the requirements or specifications.
- Make revisions, if necessary.
- Determine whether to build upon the prototype or throw it away.
- Document the prototype.

Quality Review

A quality review session is an informal session held with colleagues to review output prior to a product's release. The key word is informal. It's not like a board of inquiry, staff meeting, or a checkpoint review meeting. The objective is for frank and open discussions regarding output and deliverables.

To hold an effective quality review session, remember the following points.

- Keep the number of attendees small. Ideally, you want seven to nine attendees, which is not too small or too large to inhibit discussion and still provides opportunities for different opinions.
- Keep the sessions short. Limit them to one or two hours. If the session must go longer, break it into smaller segments to be held at different times.
- Evaluate the output, not the individual. The purpose of a quality review session is to identify shortcomings of the product, not people. All attendees should recognize that this is *the spirit of the session*. If anyone feels otherwise, personalities will clash, and nothing will be accomplished other than drawing battle lines.
- Limit attendance by peers. Under no circumstances should management attend. The reason for this is that other attendees, including the developer of the product, may feel they are being evaluated and will be less inclined to speak their minds.
- Take notes, not minutes, on ideas that may improve the product. In fact, you may want to revise the product at the review session. However, the best approach is to record all suggestions, return to your desk, and incorporate those ideas that have merit.

The benefits of a quality review session are obvious. They encourage open discussion about the product, not people. They also foster a safe environment for identifying shortcomings of output and encourage creative thinking about how to overcome them.

for Conducting a Quality Review

- Determine the purpose.
- Set up the date, time, and location.
- Develop an agenda.
- Invite attendees.
- Distribute material for review in advance, if possible.
- Conduct the session.
- Take notes during the review.
- Incorporate feedback.

QUARTILES

Quartiles involve dividing a distribution of values into four equal parts. The top quartile is called the first quartile, and the bottom one is the fourth quartile.

Quartiling provides a convenient way to evaluate a distribution. It is also simple to apply.

 for Dividing a Distribution into Quartiles

- Sort the distribution into either ascending or descending order.
    - Example (using sixteen observations):

      101, 102, 103, 104, 105, 106, 107, 108, 109, 110, 111, 112, 113, 114, 115, 116

- Divide the total number of observations by four.

  16 / 4 = 4

- From the top (or left-hand side), count to the last observation in the top quartile, and draw a line.

  101, 102, 103, 104, | 105, 106, 107, 108, 109, 110, 111, 112, 113, 114, 115, 116

- From the value after the previous quartile, count the next 25 percent of the observations, and draw a line.

  101, 102, 103, 104, | 105, 106, 107, 108, | 109, 110, 111, 112, 113, 114, 115, 116

- Calculate the third quartile like the second quartile, and draw a line.

  101, 102, 103, 104, | 105, 106, 107, 108, | 109, 110, 111, 112, | 113, 114, 115, 116

    - Note: The remainder will be the fourth quartile.

RECYCLE AND RESALE

Think about your office. If it's like most offices, opportunities exist for recycling. Here is a short list of items that you could recycle: copier paper, cardboard boxes, and aluminum cans as well as parts from copiers, microcomputers, and other office equipment.

Some firms recycle items like those above, not so much as to recoup expenditures but to raise funds for charitable causes. By doing so, the firm gains goodwill as well as money.

In addition to recycling, a firm can sell nondisposable items to recoup expenditures, such as furniture and equipment. It can sell these items to employees or to the public as well as give them to a charitable institution.

The benefits of recycle and resale are obvious. It saves resources, including money. It also reduces inventory and can reduce taxes. Finally, it can be good public relations.

 for Recycle and Resale

- Look in cluttered areas.
- Look in storage areas and cabinets.
- Identify items that have not been touched in awhile.
- Identify items that have become less important or obsolescent due to new technology.

REENGINEERING

Reengineering, in contrast to total quality improvement, involves radical change. The idea behind reengineering is to develop and implement a new process, capitalizing on technology *enablers* and breakthrough opportunities.

To perform reengineering, a project team is formed. The team focuses on a major change, requiring large investments of time, labor, and effort. The reengineering project deals with a complex set of issues in a high-risk environment.

Reengineering offers several benefits if it succeeds. When a better process is put in place, it can provide dramatic gains in productivity. It can also improve the competitive position of the firm. Further, it increases the global perspective of employees because reengineering requires participants to understand the existing and new processes.

 for Performing Reengineering

- Develop a project plan.
- Dedicate the team members to the project.
- Seek concurrence on a standard modeling technique and tool.
- Perform an in-depth risk assessment.
- Develop a thorough understanding of the existing and new process.
- Identify key players (e.g., change champion, change agent, change target).
- Have the team focus on the *to-be* rather than on the *as-is* process.

REPLANNING

Sometimes a project doesn't proceed as planned. The scope may have expanded, the complexity of work may have been greater than expected, and extraneous actions (e.g., budget cuts) may have occurred. Under these and many other circumstances, replanning may become necessary.

Replanning offers three benefits. One, it provides the opportunity to develop realistic, meaningful plans. Two, it requires project managers to keep a *finger on the pulse*, or the progress, of a project. Finally, it can generate commitment on teams that have experienced high turnover. The downsides to replanning are slowing project momentum and consuming already limited time and resources.

 for Replanning

- Identify the causes, not the symptoms, for the replanning.
- Dedicate sufficient resources (e.g., time, people, equipment, money).
- Evaluate the impact of the replanning.
- Determine which current activities can continue and which can cease.
- Obtain appropriate buy-in for the new plan from clients, senior management, and team members.
- Communicate the new plan.
- Distribute the new plan.

REPORTS

Reports play a vital role in any organization. They are primarily a communications tool for managing the performance of organizations and people.

To be effective, reports must meet certain criteria. They must serve a purpose, should contain only relevant information, and must be timely.

The benefits of well-designed reports are obvious. They provide effective communications, audit trails, and performance management.

 for Developing Reports

- Determine the purpose.
- Define the audience.
- Include a title, legend, date, and point of contact on the report.
- Determine frequency of production.
- Determine distribution.

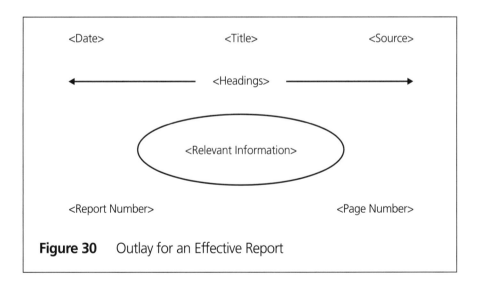

Figure 30   Outlay for an Effective Report

REQUEST FOR PROPOSAL (RESPONSE)

A request for proposal is a document that specifies requirements and expectations potential vendors must satisfy. Interested vendors then prepare a response.

Good responses to a proposal include the following characteristics. First, they cover three components: technicality (e.g., standards), management (e.g., legal), and cost (e.g., payment schedule). Second, they are written clearly. Third, they have been reviewed for accuracy and from a legal perspective. Fourth, they follow the requested format.

A well-written response to a proposal request offers two benefits. It enhances the reputation of the firm, and it encourages a teaming environment, even if the firm doesn't *win* a project.

 for Developing Responses to a Request for Proposal

- Understand the client's needs and specifications, and discern the scope of work.
- Use good project management disciplines.
- Conduct an internal capabilities-assessment.
- Conduct a risk assessment.
- Determine whether generating the proposal is in line with the strategic plan.
- Conduct internal reviews of the proposal draft.
- Make revisions.
- Submit it to the requestor.

Resource Leveling

Quite often, an office or business operates with too few or too many people. Too few people causes existing staff to *spread themselves too thin,* resulting in superficial work and missed deadlines; too many people causes operating costs to increase and produces decreased gains in productivity. Ideally, you want an optimum level of people. Resource leveling is the way to achieve that optimum level.

Resource leveling is a method that reduces the peaks of having too many people and the valleys of having too few people in an organization or a project. In other words, it enables having a steady workforce available to meet needs.

In addition, resource leveling eliminates the hiring and firing of people as well as the amount of time, effort, and expense associated with that endeavor. You can then apply those savings in time, effort, and expense to more productive activities.

A histogram illustrates how well an organization uses its people. Actually, there are two types of histograms, unleveled and leveled. An unleveled histogram displays extensive variations between peaks and valleys. A leveled histogram—which is what you hope to achieve—reflects minimal peaks and valleys.

You can convert an unleveled histogram into a leveled one by shortening or lengthening the flow time or total hours to complete a task. This process is called leveling because you try to smooth the profile of the histogram.

 for Resource Leveling

- For each task, determine the flow time and total hours to complete it.
- Assign people to each task, identifying the hours per day (or whatever units and increments you choose) to work on it.
- Draw an x-axis (horizontal line) to reflect the time scale (e.g., days, weeks).
- Draw a y-axis (vertical line) to reflect cumulative time (e.g., hours).

- Plot the cumulative hours for a given period (e.g., day) by first locating the day on the x-axis and the number of hours working that day on the y-axis.
  - Note: You repeat this step until you identify all occurrences of work.
- Look at the resulting histogram to identify peaks and valleys.
  - Note: The areas with the steepest differences in peaks and valleys are the best candidates for making reassignments.
- Change, or level, the histogram by modifying the hours per day the person(s) works and replotting the results until the differences in peaks and valleys are less.

Task	Name	Flowtime (days)	Total Hours	Hours to Work/Day
Design	Jim (J)	4	20	5
Test	Ted (T)	3	24	8
Implement	Ted (T)	2	16	8

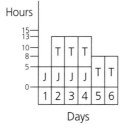

Unleveled (per task assignments above)

Leveled (if tasks are rearranged)

Figure 31   Resource Leveling for Tool Shop L

RESPONSIBILITY MATRIX

A responsibility matrix is a method for identifying who is responsible for performing specific tasks. It may also identify the degree of responsibility for each task.

A responsibility matrix is no good, of course, if it isn't distributed to the people who must do the work. It might be useful to *broadcast* the matrix to ensure visibility, and consequently, commitment.

The responsibility matrix offers several advantages. It engenders accountability, especially after giving everybody on the project a copy, and it improves coordination because everybody knows the responsibilities. Finally, it gives everyone visibility for their work.

 for Developing a Responsibility Matrix

- On the left side (y-axis) of a sheet of paper, list the tasks to perform.
- Along the top (x-axis) of the page, list the names of individuals.
- When a relationship exists between a task and a person to perform it, place an *x* or some other meaningful symbol(s) to reflect that relationship.

Task	Names		
	Melissa	**Rick**	**Nicole**
Develop user manual	X	X	X
Obtain approvals	X	X	
Distribute user manuals			X

Table 14   Responsibility Matrix for Z-Software Corporation

RETURN ON INVESTMENT

The return on investment (ROI) assumes that once all the costs have been recovered for a product, service, and so forth, it can then start generating a profitable rate of return.

To calculate the ROI, some information must be available, such as implementation and operating costs as well as the expected rate of return in the first year. The resulting value is the return on investment for the first year, which is calculated by subtracting the operating and implementation costs from the expected return. The ROI is then calculated for the subsequent years that the product or service will be in effect. The approach is to sum the expected return on investment generated for each year.

The benefits of the ROI are that it helps to determine whether to make the selected investment or to invest it somewhere else.

 for Calculating the Return on Investment

- For the first year, calculate the return on investment by subtracting the operating and implementation costs from the expected amount.
  - Example:

Money Generated in the First Year		$100,000
Operating Costs	–	20,000
Implementation Costs	–	50,000
Return on Investment		$ 30,000

- For each subsequent year in the life of the product, service, and so on, subtract the operating costs from the expected amount of return, if applicable.

  - Example:

Expected Rate of Return for the First Year	$ 5,000 *
Expected Rate of Return for the Second Year	+ 10,000 **
Expected Rate of Return for the Third Year	+ 15,000 **
Return on Investment	$30,000

    * Return minus operating and implementation costs
    ** Return minus operating costs

- Determine whether to invest in the product, service, and so on, or to invest the money somewhere else (e.g., bank savings account).

REUSE

Reinventing the wheel doesn't always make sense. It takes time and effort away from concentrating on more important issues and problems. It also wastes resources. Reuse is a tool for eliminating the tendency to reinvent the wheel. Reuse is using the components of a product, process, or system that have been successfully developed and applied in the past. Items of frequent reuse are software, documentation, data, hardware, processes, and procedures.

For reuse to occur successfully, certain conditions must exist. There must be a cataloging of items to reuse. There must also be standards set for the components themselves and their interfaces (e.g., standards for the exchange of data), and there must be good documentation about each component.

The advantages to reuse are many. It saves time, effort, and money. It also increases productivity and speed of delivery and improves both quality and communication.

 for Reuse

- Identify the components for reuse.
- Establish standards for the components and their interfaces.
- Put the components under configuration control.
- Document the components and their interfaces.
- Set up a reuse library or repository.
- Identify conditions for reusing specific components.

RISK MANAGEMENT

Risks, or vulnerabilities, are always present. There are many categories and levels of risk, each with its own probability of occurrence and level of impact.

There are essentially four elements to risk management, and their relationships are cyclical: risk identification, risk analysis, risk control, and risk reporting.

Risk identification involves identifying the risks, components, and processes potentially affected. *Risk analysis* is converting information gathered into identification. *Risk control* is identifying controls that are or should be in place to deal with a threat. *Risk reporting* is reporting on the results of the risk identification, analysis, and control.

Risk management offers many benefits. It allows for knowing the strengths and weaknesses of a project, product, process, or system. It also enables knowing what measures are in place to deal with risks, and it helps in identifying the probability and impact of a threat. Finally, it gives advance warning about a threat and provides time to prepare for its impact.

 for Risk Management

- Understand the project, product, process, or systems as thoroughly as possible.
- Develop a list of components.
- Develop a list of threats and their applicability to each component.
- Prioritize threats and components.
- Identify probabilities of occurrence and impacts.
- Identify controls that are in place and should be in place.
- For controls that are inadequate or nonexistent, determine what actions to take.
- Prepare findings and recommendations.

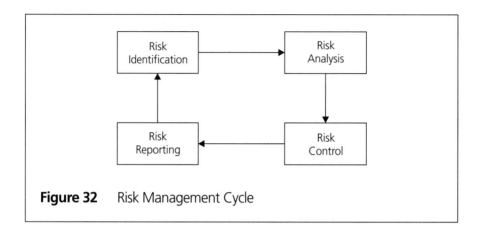

Figure 32   Risk Management Cycle

SAMPLING

Sampling is examining an entire population based upon the collection of data from a subset of that population. The idea is that by taking a sample, you can make inferences about the entire population.

Sampling can be random or purposeful. Random sampling occurs when every item in the population has an equal chance of being selected. Purposeful sampling is using a specific criterion (e.g., everyone with blue eyes) to select an item.

Samples can be segmented according to some grouping and class. Samples can also be taken from homogeneous and heterogeneous populations. When sampling from a heterogeneous population, however, homogeneity can be obtained through subdivisions (e.g., sex and race).

Regardless of the type of sampling, reliable sampling has three common characteristics. First, the sample is randomly selected. Second, the sample must be representative of the population. Third, bias should be minimized.

Sampling is more beneficial than examining an entire population because it is cheaper and faster and has a history of success behind it. Furthermore, it can be automated and can be used in a wide variety of environments.

 for Sampling

- Determine the population to sample.
- Determine the desired confidence level.
- Determine the size of the sample.
- Define the class intervals, if applicable.
- Use a random number table to select the first sample.
- Determine the type of sample.
- Develop inferences from the results.

SCATTERGRAM

The scattergram is a graph that identifies the relationship between two variables. It consists of an x-axis (horizontal), a y-axis (vertical), and plots that reflect instances of axial relationships.

The scattergram offers several benefits. It is not only easy to build, but it is also easy to interpret. It can also show the relationship between two variables and can identify anomalies. Finally, it can identify the measure of central tendency, or average.

 for Building and Interpreting a Scattergram

- Identify the two variables.
- Draw the x- and y-axes, reflecting cumulative graduations of scale.
- Record the instances of the relationship between the two variables.
- Plot the data.
- Draw a line that bisects the main body of the plots to reflect the average.
    - Note: Observe all anomalies (plots outside the main body).
- Conduct further research to identify the contributors to the average and the anomalies.

Tools and Tips for Today's Project Manager

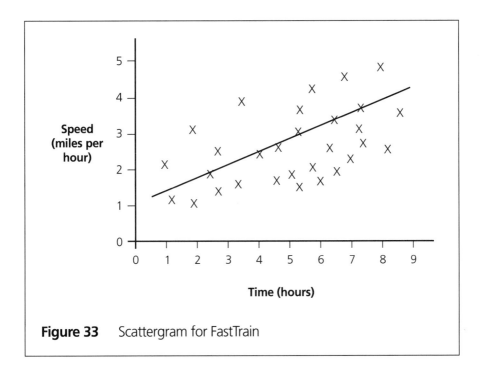

Figure 33   Scattergram for FastTrain

SCIENTIFIC METHOD

The scientific method has been around for centuries. Today, it remains a useful tool for developing new ideas and other concepts and testing them for verification and validation.

The scientific method can be applied in many ways in the project environment. It can be used for analyzing, revising, and developing processes, and it can be used to generate new ideas for developing new products or processes.

The scientific method offers several benefits. It provides a disciplined approach for solving problems and has a history of success behind it. It also works well with other business tools and techniques. Finally, it is modifiable to accommodate for different environments.

 for Applying the Scientific Method

- Develop an idea, concept, and so on.
- Collect facts (e.g., survey).
- Summarize the facts (e.g., frequency distribution).
- Develop an explanation for the facts found (e.g., model).
- Conduct a test of the explanation (e.g., verification of the model).

S Curve

The S curve is a line chart that shows the planned versus actual cumulative costs for a project. The difference between the planned and the actual lines plotted on the chart indicates a positive or negative cost performance. Ideally, the planned and actual should match. The S curve can be plotted for individual groups of tasks or for an entire project.

The S curve offers several benefits. It allows you to determine the overall cost performance for a task, resource, or entire project. It also provides the means for anticipating potential cost problems in the future. Finally, it provides an audit trail on the overall performance of a project.

 for Constructing and Using an S Curve

- Draw a horizontal line (x-axis) reflecting a time continuum (e.g., days, months).
- Draw a vertical line (y-axis) reflecting the graduated cumulative costs for your project.
- Plot the planned cumulative cost for the project at periodic time intervals (e.g., weekly).
- Connect the planned plots using a dotted line.
- As data are accumulated, plot the cumulative cost for a specific point in time.
- Connect the actual plots using a solid line.

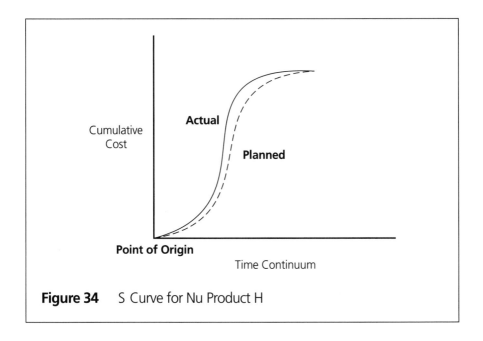

Figure 34   S Curve for Nu Product H

Tools and Tips for Today's Project Manager

SELF-DIRECTED WORK TEAMS

Self-directed work teams are multidisciplinary groups that function autonomously to accomplish a specific goal. The basis for them lies in empowering the team and granting decision-making authority, with all members sharing the responsibility for the results.

The benefits of self-directed work teams are that they generate a greater sense of commitment and ownership, reduce layers on management, and encourage teamwork.

 for Managing Self-Directed Work Teams

- Provide adequate training (e.g., planning, team building) for people working on self-directed work teams.
- Allow the necessary autonomy for the team to accomplish its mission.
- Procure the necessary resources for the team to accomplish its mission.
- Ensure that the team has a clear, specific goal to achieve.
- Encourage good teaming etiquette.

SINGLE POINT OF CONTACT

As organizations or projects grow in size and their processes become more complex, it becomes increasingly difficult to determine who is responsible for specific activities, procedures, or processes—other than the project manager or the person at the top of a functional organization. This results in wasted time and effort to find the right person to contact. Establishing a single point of contact, whether for an activity, procedure, process, or project, can lessen the effects of growth in size and complexity.

There are other benefits to establishing single points of contact. It encourages a sense of responsibility and accountability. It also forces managers and project managers to delegate.

 for Establishing a Single Point of Contact

- Define activities, procedures, processes, and so on.
- Assign a person as a single point of contact for a specific activity, procedure, process, and so on, or a group of activities, procedures, processes, and so on.
- Distribute the name and contact information for each single point of contact.
- Document responsibilities for each single point of contact.
- Determine the requisite level of skills and knowledge for each single point of contact.

SKETCH

A sketch is a diagram that communicates a specific idea or fact or provides an explanation. It relies on images or symbols to communicate.

A good sketch has certain characteristics. It is clear, it is concise, and it is self-explanatory to a large extent. Finally, its contents are applied consistently, even if continued on another page.

A sketch provides several benefits. It enables people to visualize the whole picture rather than only a subset. It also reduces the possibility of misunderstandings and confusion and is easier to maintain than narrative descriptions.

 for Developing a Sketch

- Identify the idea, fact, or explanation to communicate.
- Develop standard symbols to reflect the topics.
- Use symbols consistently.
- Add a legend.
- Keep sketches uncongested by having no more than ten components on a page.
- If placed on a transparency, make sure the contents can be viewed easily by the audience.

SOFTWARE SELECTION

Software tools, or packages, are tremendous productivity aids. They help to process large volumes of data, and they perform repetitive functions and complex calculations. Unfortunately, little forethought is given to the acquisition of software. A package is purchased, loaded on a computer, and then people are expected to use it. This results in frustrated users who vent their anger at the software when in reality, the problem lies with the process of selecting the package.

Any software selection should be methodical; that is, it should have a logical flow. Specifically, it should define what features are needed, who the package is for, when will it be available, how it will be used, and even where (e.g., the computer) it will be employed. The selection should be objective and should satisfy the needs of the users.

A software selection process provides four benefits. One, it provides a consistent approach for selecting software. Two, it provides users with software that meets their needs. Three, it reduces the chances of unwanted software just sitting on a shelf. Four, it reduces the frustration that people experience with new software.

 for Software Selection Process

- Identify requirements and specifications (e.g., type of hardware, compatibility, user-friendliness, functionality, help-desk services).
- Use an objective approach for selecting software (e.g., weighted selection criteria approach).
- Test the software against requirements and specifications.
- Provide adequate training for a smoother transition.
- Expect a learning curve, even after training.
- Evaluate multiple products from multiple vendors rather than just selecting from a preferred vendor.

SPAN OF CONTROL

Span of control is a theory that says a person can control seven to ten people effectively. Span of control is important if you are a project manager because you may have to appoint *leads* to supervise other team members.

You can have wide and narrow spans of control. Ideally, you want an optimum level, somewhere between high and low. Beyond ten people, the degree of control degrades. A wide span of control entails controlling a large amount of people. On organization chart, it appears like a flat pancake with a bubble on top of it. The bubble, of course, is the person in charge, and the remainder are the people supporting him.

Effective span of control offers two advantages. It provides the right level of overseeing. It also ensures the efficient and effective use of resources.

 for Developing an Effective Span of Control

- Identify the number of people on the team.
- Evaluate the leadership qualities of the individuals.
- Divide the team into subgroups, not to exceed ten people and no less than two.
- Assign individuals with the best leadership qualities as *leads* over a subgroup.

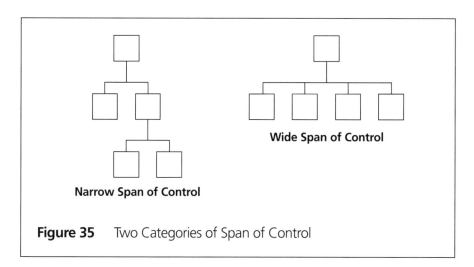

Narrow Span of Control

Wide Span of Control

Figure 35   Two Categories of Span of Control

SPEED-READING

In an area of information overload, it is difficult to find what is important. Fortunately, speed-reading is one tool for doing just that.

The keys to speed-reading are not reading word-by-word or perusing illustrations. The keys are identifying the main ideas and the logical flow of the document. Then, if necessary, you can revisit sections for additional information.

Speed-reading offers several benefits. Important information and ideas can be located quickly, and it enables better use of time. It also expedites the learning curve.

 for Speed-Reading

- Skim through the entire document, getting a feel for its overall structure and tone.

- While skimming, notice the headings and subtitles to get an understanding of the subject matter.

- While skimming, notice the illustrations, charts, diagrams, and so on, for information content.

- Peruse the introduction and conclusion first to obtain general information about the subject.

- When perusing pages, avoid reading one word at a time and looking at footnotes.

- Traverse the center of the document, noticing key words and phrases.

STAFF MEETINGS

A staff meeting is a regularly scheduled session where people assemble to receive and distribute information and share knowledge and experiences. Like other meetings, it requires good planning and organization prior to holding it and effective management while being conducted.

An effective staff meeting has certain characteristics. It has one or more objectives to achieve. It also follows a planned pattern, specifically topic and time frames, and has a positive atmosphere. Finally, it encourages participation from everyone.

A good staff meeting offers several benefits. It builds *esprit de corps* and resolves potential misunderstandings and conflicts. It also enables sharing of knowledge, information, and expertise.

 for Holding Successful Staff Meetings

- Identify the participants.
- Develop and distribute a *standardized* agenda that can be tailored for each meeting.
- Hold the meetings at regular intervals—at the same time and location, if possible.
- Keep meetings short.
- Encourage information sharing.
- Allow everyone the opportunity to participate.
- Take minutes or notes.
- Publish the minutes or notes.

STANDARDS

A standard is a level of performance that communicates specific expectations when conducting business. Unlike guidelines, standards require compliance. Compliance to standards sometimes generates fear. Although the fear is understandable, it is groundless if a standard is clear, measurable, definable, easily applied, objective, recordable, and accessible.

A misconception exists that control must exist over all activities within an organization. Not only is this impossible, but it also leads to overcontrol. Standards should only exist when necessary.

Standards are beneficial because they provide an objective means for measuring performance. They also communicate expectations of performance and provide uniformity when conducting business. Finally, they ensure a minimum, expected level of performance.

 for Developing Standards

- Determine the goal(s) of the standard.
- Gather input from key individuals during the development of the standard.
- Develop the standard based upon the input.
- Seek feedback from key individuals.
- Develop the standard.
- Document the standard.
- Obtain *buy off* on the standard.
- Communicate the standard.

STATEMENT OF WORK (UNDERSTANDING)

The statement of work (SOW), more informally known as a statement of understanding, is an agreement among the project manager, senior management, and the client. It describes—at a high level—what is to be built; the major milestone dates, responsibilities, assumptions, and constraints; and desired qualities of the final product.

The SOW offers four benefits. One, it encourages communication and, consequently, reduces misunderstandings. Two, it addresses assumptions early in the project. Three, it generates commitment by all three parties. Finally, it provides agreed-upon baselines to evaluate performance.

 for Developing a Statement of Work (Understanding)

- Identify the major parties.
- Negotiate in good faith.
- Identify the major contents.
- Provide spaces for signatures or initials.
- Occasionally, revisit the SOW to gauge progress and determine need for renegotiation.

I. **Introduction**
II. **Assumptions**
   A. Purpose
   B. Scope
   C. Background
III. **Constraints**
IV. **Schedule Considerations**
V. **Cost and Budget Considerations**
VI. **Quality Considerations**
VII. **Responsibilities**
VIII. **Amendments**
IX. **Signatures**

Figure 36 Outline for a Statement of Work (Understanding)

STATISTICAL CORRUPTIONS AND DISTORTIONS

From time to time, statistics are calculated and flashed around without any thought about their level of accuracy. Sometimes, too, they are intentionally misused to support a particular viewpoint or action.

Some statistics, for example, are cited without knowing the individual biases that went into the development of the statistics or the institutional influences that may have heavily influenced the results. Some statistics about a narrow population are used to make inferences about a whole population. The assumption or intent is that a statistic can be generalized. Some statistics may have been calculated incorrectly, thereby providing inaccurate results.

The benefits of identifying the potential statistical corruptions and distortions are twofold. First, it halts propagating bad information that can lead to faulty conclusions in a study. Two, it leads to more accurate decisions because a decision-maker knows the weaknesses in the data being used.

 for Identifying Statistical Corruptions and Distortions

- Determine the purpose of the data that will be used.
- Identify the developers of the data.
- Contact the developers of the data, if possible, to obtain the assumptions and statistical approach used.
- If corruptions and distortions were used, determine the disposition of the statistic (e.g., use it with caveats, discard it).

STATISTICAL PROCESS CONTROL CHART

A statistical process control (SPC) chart graphically displays data about some process or product. The data, based upon samples or observations, are collected over a period of time. The data, when plotted, should fall within an acceptable range, or tolerance level. Any data falling outside that range may indicate a problem or an opportunity for improvement.

A SPC chart provides several benefits. It provides for effective monitoring of processes. It also helps to identify problems when they arise. Further, it aids in capitalizing on anomalies that may, in fact, lead to better processes or products.

 for Developing a Statistical Process Control Chart

- Draw an x-axis (horizontal line) to reflect a time continuum (e.g., months).
- Draw a y-axis (vertical line) for a variable (e.g., measurement criteria).
- Draw a line perpendicular to the y-axis to reflect the mean or average of the variable.
  - Note: The mean may be based on your knowledge, experience, or statistical calculation.
- Draw a dotted line perpendicular to the y-axis to reflect the upper control limit.
- Draw a dotted line perpendicular to the y-axis to reflect the lower control limit.
  - Note: Both the upper and lower control limits represent the acceptable range; anything outside the lines represents anomalies or deviations.
- Plot occurrences over a period of time.
- Identify anomalies for further analysis.

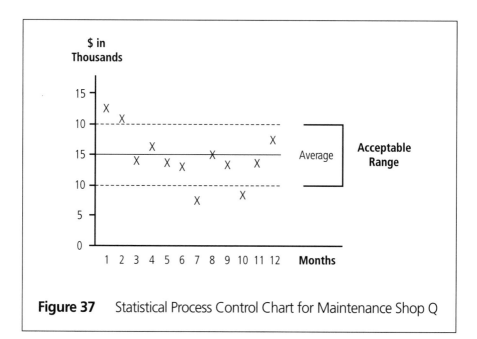

Figure 37   Statistical Process Control Chart for Maintenance Shop Q

Tools and Tips for Today's Project Manager

STATUS COLLECTION

Status collection is an action that you take to determine the progress made in achieving your plans, but this action is filled with pitfalls that can hinder the validity of your feedback.

First, you face a lack of available information. Unless you have some mechanism in place to receive regular feedback, you will have to seek it. Holding meetings, interviewing people, and observing work are three ways to obtain feedback.

Second, you occasionally deal with defensive people. They will resist any effort to provide the feedback that you need. When facing these people, seek other sources of information, such as talking with other colleagues.

Third, you deal with untruthful people, who will tell you anything to *get you off their backs*. For instance, you talk with someone regarding a specific task, and you ask how much he has completed. Early in the project he replies, "I'm 90 percent done," but much later, he never finishes the task on time or within budget. That's known as the *90 percent syndrome*—that is, people rattling off status so they'll be left alone for whatever reason.

You can overcome these and other obstacles by following a few simple guidelines.

- Stay objective. Avoid giving the impression that all you want to hear is positive feedback; you will hear only what you want to hear and not what you need to hear.
- Make your assessments after you receive all the facts. Armed with complete information, you can make a rational decision.
- Collect status regularly. People can predict when you'll need feedback and can prepare accordingly.
- Document your findings and the logic behind your final assessment. In doing so, you will not only have a historical document for future reference but also an understanding of how your project got to where it is today.

for Conducting a Meaningful Status Collection

- Determine the means for status collection.
- Determine the format of the data.
- Identify the sources of data.
- *Cleanse* the data.
- Set up regular intervals for collecting data.
- Collect the data.

STATUS REVIEW MEETINGS

Occasionally, you will want to know how well you're progressing according to the plan that you developed for your project. You can do that by conducting a status review meeting.

A status review meeting is a regularly scheduled session where the people working on a project give feedback on progress to date regarding cost, schedule, and quality.

Like other meetings, it requires good planning and organization prior to holding it and effective management while being conducted.

An effective status review meeting has certain characteristics. The right people attend, particularly the people responsible for the work being performed. It provides time for open dialogue to discuss key business and technical areas with respect to meeting cost, schedule, and quality criteria. Finally, it provides the grounds for effective assessment of a situation or project.

The biggest advantage of a status review meeting is that it helps you stay abreast of what people are doing on your project and how well they are doing it. It also communicates to people that you're serious about your project and that you hold them accountable for their performance.

 for Conducting Effective Status Review Meetings

- Determine exactly what to cover at the meeting.
- Identify all the participants.
- Develop and distribute a standardized agenda that can be tailored for each meeting.
- Hold the meetings at regular intervals—at the same time and location, if possible.
- Remain objective by focusing on the facts and data, not on the people.

SUPPLY CHAIN MANUFACTURING

First came material requirement planning (MRP). Then came manufacturing resource planning (MRP II) followed by just-in-time (JIT) manufacturing. Now, there's supply chain manufacturing (SCM). SCM is a comprehensive, integrated manufacturing approach using leading-edge technologies to produce and deliver goods and services to the customer.

Unlike MRP, MRP II, and JIT, SCM looks at all processes and players as an integrated system. Working closely with suppliers and customers, a manufacturer produces based upon *pull* (customer-driven) rather than *push* (manufacturer-driven) considerations.

All the disciplines (e.g., logistics, engineering, procurement, finance, manufacturing) are an integrated unit. It is this integration and scope that gives SCM its distinctive character.

The benefits of SCM are many. It can still employ the tools and techniques of MRP, MRP II, and JIT. It also capitalizes on the use of the newest technology (e.g., the Internet) and builds a closer relationship with both suppliers and customers. Furthermore, it requires teamwork among all the disciplines and reduces inventory, particularly just-in-case inventory.

 for Applying Supplier Chain Manufacturing

- Identify all the suppliers, customers, and functional participants (e.g., logisticians).
- Identify all the processes (e.g., engineering).
- Develop models of the entire manufacturing operation.
- Identify which areas (e.g., inventory, handling, planning, production) of the supply chain leverage the use of new information technologies (e.g., Internet tools).
- Develop a close relationship with suppliers and customers that includes sharing information about inventory and planned production.

SWAT TEAMS

The SWAT team concept is taken from the police response teams that deal with emergency situations. These teams are called special weapons and tactics—hence, SWAT. In project management, SWAT teams are used to create and set up the infrastructure for a new project under the aegis of a project manager. These teams develop and implement plans (e.g., work breakdown structure, schedule), and then a *normal* project team replaces the SWAT team.

The benefits of using SWAT teams are threefold. One, they can get a project up and running early. Two, they can clarify assumptions and issues early. Three, they can shorten the life cycle of a project. The downsides are that SWAT team members can burn out, and using a SWAT team decreases ownership among the permanent replacements.

 for Using SWAT Teams

- Identify specific goals and deliverables for the team.
- Ensure that ownership by client and replacement project team members exists.
- Ensure that the SWAT team documents its efforts.
- Create a smooth transition when passing the project infrastructure from the SWAT team to its successor.
- Ensure that the replacement team understands the output of the SWAT team.

SYSTEMS THEORY

Financial, computer, missile, and other systems, such as the ecosystem, are all ways to view something as a set of elements interacting to produce output. This viewpoint is called systems theory, and it can help you to understand how your organization or work environment operates.

System theory entails viewing an entity, such as an organization, as consisting of several elements. You must identify those elements to understand your working environment.

The basic elements of a system are:

- participants (e.g., people, machinery, organizations) who make decisions or receive inputs, outputs, or both
- processes (e.g., activities, procedures that transform or transfer inputs or outputs or both)
- inputs (e.g., data, triggers) that enable processes to occur
- outputs (e.g., data, products) that result from the execution of processes
- boundaries (e.g., internal and external points with the environment and other systems).

Systems theory offers two main benefits. It will provide you with a better understanding of your work environment. With it, you can also reduce the complexity of the environment and concentrate on what matters.

 for Applying Systems Theory

- Draw symbols (e.g., circles) for the major functions or processes that occur.
- Draw symbols (e.g., boxes) reflecting the major *actors* or *players*.
- Draw lines connecting a process with another process(es), actor with another actor(s), and process(es) with actor(s).
- Label the lines to indicate what flows (e.g., forms, information) between symbols.
- Add a legend at the bottom of the page.

T Account Decision-Making

Some business professionals toss dice to help them make a difficult decision. Others rely upon intuition. The best approach, however, is to come to a decision using some logical process. One method is to use T account decision-making. T account decision-making entails listing and weighing the advantages and disadvantages, then summing the weight for each alternative and selecting the best one.

T account decision-making is beneficial because it is simple and quick and provides a structured approach for making a decision.

 for Performing T Account Decision-Making

- Draw a large *t* on a sheet of paper or use computer software to create one.
- On the left side, list advantages.
- On the right side, list disadvantages.
- Leave a blank column on the far right to calculate the *differences*.
- Assign a weight for each advantage, such as four points for a great advantage and zero points for no advantage.
- Assign a weight for each disadvantage, such as four points for a great disadvantage and zero points for no disadvantage.
- Sum both columns and subtract the total score of the disadvantages from that of the advantages.
  - Note: A positive result means the advantages outweigh the disadvantages. A negative result means the opposite.

BUILD NEW COMPLEX					
Advantages		**Disadvantages**		**Difference**	
Weight	Item	Weight	Item		
4	Tax Write-Off	3	Costly to Build		
4	Larger Facility	2	High Property Tax Area		
3	Convenient Location				
Total 11		5		**11–5=6**	

Table 15   T Account Decision-Making Chart for R Construction Corporation

TEAMWORK

Building teamwork is no simple task. It requires that mechanisms be in place to enable everyone on the team to *synergize*, meaning the combined energies are greater than the sum of individual actions. However, you must make synergy happen.

Effective teams have these ten characteristics:

1. A definable mission.

2. Fewer than ten people.

3. Autonomy, or the latitude to make decisions regarding the team's destiny within the scope of the mission of parent organizations.

4. Resources to accomplish missions.

5. Reasonable deadlines to accomplish goals.

6. A record of activities.

7. Team members who understand expectations of performance.

8. Patience.

9. Participation from everyone.

10. A leader.

Teamwork offers many obvious advantages. It encourages communication, builds trust, and facilitates coordination. It also increases individual and group effectiveness and improves efficiency.

 for Teamwork

- Define the mission of the team.
- Limit membership to no more than ten people.
- Set a deadline for completing the mission.
- Have people on the team participate in determining how to complete the mission.
- Ensure that the resulting plan is communicated to everyone on the team.
- Ensure that team members understand their roles and realize their impact on the results of the team's efforts.
- Appoint a leader commensurate with the style of the team.

TELECOMMUTING

Telecommuting is working from home for an employer. It is a major contributor to the virtual office concept because it applies Web technology, groupware, mobile computing, and distributed computing architecture. As office space becomes more expensive and traffic congestion more prevalent, telecommuting will grow in popularity.

Telecommuting offers three benefits. One, it reduces the need for office space. Two, it empowers people. Three, it generates accountability for results. Its challenges are providing adequate technical equipment and support and obtaining a willingness to alter managerial styles to accommodate the new working environment.

 for Telecommuting

- Provide adequate technical support.
- Provide adequate hardware, software, and telecommunications.
- Use deliverable-based management.
- Conduct periodic follow-up with telecommuters.
- Employ different modes of communication (e.g., pager, microcomputer, telephone).
- Establish *core days* whereby telecommuters work together one or more days at a central office.
- Provide flexibility in scheduling work hours and days.

TELEPHONE TAG

You're off to meetings. You may be walking about the shop floor. You may be attending a seminar. Meanwhile, people are trying to contact you, but you're unavailable. Upon returning to the office, you try to call these people back, and they are not in! This is called telephone tag.

Combating telephone tag provides several obvious benefits. It saves time and, consequently, money. It also increases productivity, and it creates more time and energy for focusing on priorities. Finally, it reduces the annoyance and frustration that comes with telephone tag.

 ## for Overcoming Telephone Tag

- Restrict your availability for receiving calls to certain times in a day.
- Have someone, like a secretary, set up appointments for you.
- Use voice mail or E-mail, if available.
- Leave an alternate number where you can be reached via a secretary, voice mail, pager, or cellular phone.
- Carry a pager or cellular phone to communicate with whomever wants to talk to you.

TESTING

Testing is the process of applying criteria against a product to determine errors or defects. The criteria, tools, and approach are the key elements of the testing process.

The criteria usually consist of the customer's requirements, specifications, and industry standards. Tools may be manual (e.g., physical inspection) or automated (e.g., software). The approach can be black box or white box.

Black box testing is focusing on inputs and outputs but not on the internal workings of the device. *White box testing* is looking at the internal, intricate workings of the product as well as the inputs and outputs.

Good testing should have certain characteristics to ensure objective, reliable, and valid results. Testing should use definitive criteria. It should also follow a plan and should have ample *cans* to test against. Further, it should be done by someone outside the product's development, and it should seek to find, not avoid, errors.

Testing offers several benefits. It provides the customer with a product of higher quality, giving the customer a feeling of confidence when using the product and the developer a feeling of confidence when delivering the product. By testing a product, it lessens the opportunity for embarrassment or legal problems.

 for Testing

- Determine the product to test.
- Determine all requirements and specifications.
- Determine the test cases.
- Develop a test plan.
- Determine the tool(s) to conduct testing.
- Determine the approach.
- Execute the tests.
- Record the results.
- Evaluate the results.
- Retest, if necessary, or modify the product and then retest.

TIME LOG

Sometimes people aren't aware of how they spend their time, whether at home or the office. One way to avoid wasting time is to record how you have been using it. The medium to do that is the time log.

Using the time log, you record what events occurred, at what time, and for how long a period of time during the day. To extract meaningful information from a time log, be sure to take several recordings at random time periods. That way, you will have a more realistic view of how well you or other people use time.

You now have information that tells you much. It tells you when your peak periods are, the types of interruptions you receive, and your slowest work moments and how you spend them. Using this information, you can take several actions. One, you can adjust your workflow so that it's more even and the work peaks are lower. Two, you can identify the interruptions that you receive and the best way to work around them. Three, you can develop performance standards for yourself and other people.

A time log offers several obvious benefits. It leads to identifying better ways to use time. It also provides information for streamlining operations and using resources more efficiently. It can even provide an audit trail for work that was done.

 for Developing and Using a Time Log

- Determine the reasons for using the log.
- Determine the length of time for collecting information.
- On the top of a sheet of paper or using computer software, compose the words *event, time,* and *duration.*
- Select randomly the intervals to record information about the events.
- Compile and analyze the data.

Event	Time	Duration (hours)
Find and fix electical short in Machine 1	8 A.M.	3
Replace servomotor in Machine 2	11 A.M.	1
Determine cause of air conditioning power surge and fix	12:30 P.M.	4

Table 16   Time Log for Repair Shop M

TOTAL QUALITY MANAGEMENT

Total quality management (TQM), also referred to as total quality control (TQC), is a comprehensive approach for improving processes to satisfy the customers' needs, specifications, and so forth.

One of the fundamental principles of TQM is focusing on the customer. Other principles include exercising continuous improvement of processes, relying on facts and data to make improvements, documenting processes, obtaining employee involvement (especially key people involved with the processes), and maintaining good customer-supplier relationships.

Some of the tools and techniques for doing TQM include:

- benchmarking
- data analysis
- Deming Wheel
- flowcharting
- interviewing
- statistical process control.

TQM offers several advantages. It encourages better relationships with suppliers and promotes a greater understanding of processes and the *big picture*. It also provides for continuous improvement. Finally, it encourages ownership from the people doing the work.

 for Implementing Total Quality Management

- Document processes.
- Encourage participation from the people doing the work.
- Establish standards to measure against.
- Focus on the customer (e.g., defining requirements).
- Institute cultural changes (e.g., education, training).
- Communicate the results.

TRANSACTIONAL ANALYSIS

Transactional analysis is a psychological tool that describes how people interact. It is based on three ego states: parent, child, and adult.

The *parent ego state* reflects authoritarian, or directive, feelings and actions. The *child ego state* reflects childlike feelings and actions, like crying and pouting. The *adult ego state* reflects mature feelings and actions like being cool-headed and realistic. All three ego states interact to form transactions.

Transactional analysis offers two benefits. Once it is learned, it is a relatively simple approach for detecting and diagnosing interactions. There is also a large body of knowledge behind it. The challenge of transactional analysis is that it is one of many tools for analyzing interactions. Whatever tool is used depends on the person's knowledge and mastery of the tool.

 for Using Transactional Analysis

- Identify the players.
- Define the issue or problem.
- Recognize the ego state for each player (child, parent, adult) by observing feelings and interaction.
- Develop a win-win solution for all players.

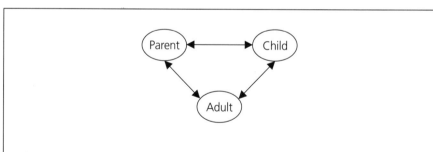

Figure 38   Ego States Relationships

TRANSPORTATION CONSOLIDATION

Transportation consolidation involves minimizing the number of trips that you have to take to accomplish a given number of tasks. If you must visit three different places, for example, you can take one trip rather than three separate ones. This takes planning, of course. You'll need to identify the sequence that you will follow in going to these locations, giving preference to their geographical outlay and the time that they are open. The key is to identify the sequence that minimizes effort and maximizes efficiency and effectiveness.

If you ever have to question which location you want to visit, prioritize the sites and then select the best spatial sequence. Quite often, spatial sequence alone will set the priority, with the most immediate location having the highest importance.

The benefits for transportation consolidation are obvious: it saves time, money, and effort.

 for Performing Transportation Consolidation

- Determine the final destination.
- Determine the intermediary steps to the final destination.
- On a sheet of paper or using computer software, draw a symbol at the top of the page representing the final destination.
- Draw symbols reflecting the intermediate stops.
- Connect the intermediate stops in a sequence that minimizes time and effort (e.g., delivery time, gas).
  - Note: You can experiment with different sequences.
- Record the approximate time of arrival, keeping in mind the time to arrive at the final destination.

Unity of Command

The unity of command principle states that a person should report to one immediate superior only. If performing as a project manager, you need to develop an organizational structure that applies this principle.

A good example of poor unity of command is a person reporting to two bosses. One boss gives direction while the other grants pay raises. Sometimes, the two bosses give contradictory signals or instructions, a circumstance that can lead to problems for the person doing the work and the managers.

Applying the unity of command principle provides three advantages. One, it reduces tension and confusion. If a person must support two superiors at the same time, a struggle will arise over whom to devote the most time. A struggle may also arise over whom to display loyalty if a conflict arises between the two superiors. Two, unity of command provides for clear reporting. A person has no question regarding who gives orders. Three, it improves decision-making. A person knows whom to ask for a decision and how to raise a concern by notifying their chain of command.

 for Unity of Command

- Identify the superiors that you are reporting to.
- Set up a joint meeting with them.
- Ask them to clarify their expectations of your performance.
- Ask them to set priorities.
- Meet jointly on a regular basis to reevaluate expectations and priorities.

VALIDITY THREATS

Collecting data is important to analyzing and evaluating processes, products, and people. It is imperative, therefore, to ensure that whatever tool is used to measure processes, services, products, or people measures what it is supposed to. Otherwise, inferences from the data could be erroneous.

A number of threats can occur that can skew or bias inferences. These include the time that the evaluation occurred, the tool or technique used, sequence of collection actions, flawed criteria, tendency to generalize from a narrow band of test, and institutional pressures.

One benefit of knowing about the possible threats to validity is that you can quantify the results of your testing or study. Another benefit is that you can take compensatory actions to offset the influences of specific validity threats.

 for Dealing with Validity Threats

- Define the goals and objectives of the study or data collection.
- Identify all the potential threats to validity.
- Prioritize those threats, and estimate their probability of occurrence.
- Determine how to account for the influences of those threats.

VALUE MANAGEMENT

Value management is similar to return on investment, or ROI, with one major difference. It incorporates intangible data into the results in addition to the more conventional cost and schedule notion.

You should understand that it is sometimes difficult to measure the value of the intangibles; however, they still hold meaning and importance. One type of analysis called psychometrics bridges this measurement gap. Psychometrics is the practical application of quantifying intangibles, i.e., being able to incorporate intangible results into a tangible analysis.

Value management offers three benefits. First, work is selected for its value, not necessarily for its financial payoff. Second, metrics are put in place before monies are allocated to start or continue work. This provides upper management with control points and measurements to better assess the value of the project as it continues through its life cycle. Nobody likes *throwing good money after bad*, especially if the value of the project has lessened. Finally, the introduction of risk factors provides a fuller picture of the evolution of the project's payoff.

 for Using Value Management

- Ensure your project is value-added before you begin requesting funding.
- Align the project's goals with corporate direction.
- Identify tangible benefits.
- Identify intangible benefits.
- Incorporate risk factors.
- Define metrics before the project begins.
- Identify control points throughout the project's life cycle.

VARIABILITY

Variability is the difference between what is expected and the actuals. Its purpose is to measure the dispersion between the two.

There are a number of calculations to determine variance: range, mean deviation, and standard deviation.

The *range* is the difference between the highest and lowest observations. The *mean deviation* is an observation's value subtracted from the mean. The *standard deviation* measures the dispersion about the mean.

The range gives the spread between the highest and lowest value. The mean deviation determines how much an observation varies from the mean. The standard deviation determines the how far individual observations are from the arithmetic mean.

 for Calculating Variability

■ The formulas for calculating all three values are:

$$\text{Range} = \text{Highest Value} - \text{Lowest Value}$$

$$\text{Mean Deviation} = \frac{\text{Sum of (Observations} - \text{Mean)}}{\text{Number of Observations}}$$

$$\text{Standard Deviation} = \sqrt{\frac{\text{Sum of (Observations} - \text{Mean)}^2}{\text{Number of Observations}}}$$

VERIFICATION

Many people in business suffer the same fate. They issue policies, procedures, reports, and other documents that preach. However, they fail to verify if their pontifications have been implemented. Quite often, they stay in their office and disregard the need for verification, assuming everyone will follow *orders*.

You can discover how well you've implemented your ideas in many ways. You can interview people. You can also collect and review statistical information or metrics to determine the impact on your organization. Or you can walk around the company and observe.

The advantages to verification are obvious. It provides an opportunity to see if linkage exists between decision and implementation. It also enables questioning whether you made a wise decision and helps you to determine whether corrective action is necessary.

 for Verification

- Determine exactly what to verify (e.g., a specific procedure).
- Gather as much background about the environment (e.g., people, organization) as possible.
- Compare the item-to-verify with what is actually occurring.
- Note deviation(s).
- Determine whether revisions are necessary to the item-to-verify or with what is actually occurring.
- Take corrective action.

VIDEOCONFERENCING

Web and PC-based technology have enabled videoconferencing to acquire a greater presence in the business environment. No longer is videoconferencing restricted to large, high-technology centers. With the right camera hardware, software, and network environment, people can talk and see others in real-time over greater distances.

Videoconferencing offers many benefits. It enables faster communications, encourages greater teamwork, and reduces opportunities for misunderstandings. Videoconferencing, however, can never replace face-to-face communications. This is because the levels of intimacy and intuition that prove useful to meetings are impossible to achieve in a videoconferencing session.

 for Using Videoconferencing

- Ensure that the technology exists at all locations.
- Use scheduled times for transmission.
- Recognize that videoconferencing is an inferior substitute for face-to-face communications.
- Keep the dialogue focused on the subject.
- Apply other technologies (e.g., whiteboards) to supplement image and audio transfers.

Viewfoils

Viewfoils, or transparencies, have become standard features at presentations. If used correctly, they can help you communicate with the audience with relative ease.

Unfortunately, many speakers have abused the use of viewfoils. They either use too many, read them while speaking, or pack them with so much information that people become confused.

Viewfoils provide obvious advantages. They can communicate information to a wide audience. They can also present information in an interesting manner. Finally, they can be used to encourage audience participation.

 for Developing Clear, Meaningful Viewfoils

- Use them sparingly.
- Use colors, but meaningfully.
- Use large print.
- Avoid cluttering.
- Give preference to graphics over text.

Virtual Teams

A virtual team is a group of people working together to achieve a common goal even though they are geographically dispersed. The advent of distributed architectures, Internet technology, groupware, and mobile computing have made virtual teams a reality.

A virtual team offers several benefits. It empowers people and reduces overhead (e.g., facilities) and layers of management.

There are three challenges regarding virtual teams. One, it requires a change in managerial philosophy, e.g., using a *deliverable-based* rather than a *task-based* management approach. Two, it requires a technical support infrastructure. Three, it requires revisions to long-standing company policies and procedures on topics like insurance coverage or work schedules.

 for Using Virtual Teams

- Provide adequate technical support.
- Revise policies and procedures.
- Have a willingness to empower people.
- Create well-defined deliverables and schedules along with meaningful performance criteria.
- Provide for opportunities for team members to congregate from time to time.

VISIBILITY WALL/ROOM

The visibility room is a communication medium for a project. The room, sometimes a wall instead, contains a wide array of information, including schedules, work breakdown structures, responsibility matrices, statistical charts, technical diagrams, financial information, and just about any information of value.

To be useful, a visibility wall or room should be well planned in advance. The focus of the outlay should be centered on the needs of the audience and the message to communicate. It should also be updated frequently to be of use.

The visibility room provides several benefits. It is an effective medium of communication, and it is an excellent place to hold meetings. Finally, it serves as a convenient place to track and monitor performance.

 for a Visibility Wall/Room

- Determine information to display.
- Sketch the layout.
- Place the information displays on the wall(s).
- Consistently update the displays.

WEB SITE

Web technology is revolutionizing the way companies in general, and even projects in particular, conduct business. A distributed computing architecture, along with user-friendly software (e.g., browsers) and cheaper, more powerful hardware, make Web sites easier to create and maintain.

A Web site, whether for an intranet or the Internet, offers three benefits. One, it provides easier access to information. Two, it encourages greater communication among people. Three, it provides visibility of a product, service, or project.

To maximize the benefits of a Web site, it must address a specific need of a specific audience and must be kept current.

 ## for Building and Maintaining a Web Site

- Define the purpose and audience for the Web site.
- Use audio and graphics to support, not replace, the main purpose.
- Provide the necessary hardware and software to optimize performance.
- Use good grammar and spelling.
- Provide addresses, phone numbers, and contact names.
- Keep links current.

WEIGHTED SELECTION CRITERIA APPROACH

The weighted selection criteria approach is an objective way to prioritize alternatives and select the best one based upon the highest score. The goal is to remove as much subjectivity as possible from the decision.

This approach involves listing requirements, assigning a point value to each one, and assigning a weighted value to each one. Next, for each requirement, multiply the assigned point value by the weighted value. Finally, add all the calculated points for each alternative. The total points will determine the relative importance of one task vis-à-vis another.

The weighted selection criteria approach offers two benefits. It is easy to use, although it is time-consuming, and it provides an objective approach for selecting the best alternative.

 for Using the Weighted Selection Criteria Approach

- List the requirements for selecting the best alternative.
- Assign a point value for each requirement.
- Assign a weighted point value to each requirement.
- For each requirement, multiply the point value by the weighted value.
- For each alternative, sum the products in the column.
- Select the alternative with the highest score.

Requirement	Point Value	ALTERNATIVE #1		ALTERNATIVE #2		ALTERNATIVE #3	
		Weighted Value	Total Value	Weighted Value	Total Value	Weighted Value	Total Value
A	4	5	20	3	12	5	20
B	8	0	0	5	40	5	40
C	10	3	30	3	30	5	50
D	5	5	25	5	25	5	25
E	3	0	0	0	0	5	15
		Total	75		107		150

Where: 5 = Meets Necessary Requirement

3 = Meets Desired but Not Necessary Requirement

0 = Does Not Meet Requirement at All

WORK BREAKDOWN STRUCTURE

Quite often, people handle a project without approaching it in a manageable, logical way. Instead, they jump in only to find that the effort was much greater than they had anticipated. They could have avoided the shock if they had developed a work breakdown structure.

A work breakdown structure is a top-down listing of tasks, moving from broad to specific, in a manner similar to an outline. Each task, for example, is expanded into subtasks; each subtask can then be expanded into greater detail, such as steps.

You can unfold a work breakdown structure into many different layers, and the more detailed the work breakdown structure, the better. The more detail, the easier it is to track progress.

A detailed work breakdown structure offers several advantages. It engenders accountability on a project because you can assign specific tasks to individuals supporting you in the work breakdown structure. It also serves as the basis for developing realistic time estimates and schedules, and it lessens the chance of duplicate effort because everyone knows exactly what to do. Finally, it forces thinking about what you'll do prior to beginning your project.

 for Developing a Work Breakdown Structure

- On a sheet of paper or using computer software, write the overall product to develop or service to provide.
- Just below the overall product or service, list the components.
  - Note: Use only one or two words.
- Under each component, list the tasks to build it.
  - Note: Use an action verb and object in the description.
- Use a numbering scheme to uniquely identify each element in the work breakdown structure, which will also indicate the relationships among elements.

1.0 Marketing Plan

　1.1 Describe the service

　1.2 Describe the market

　　　1.2.1 Identify competitors

　　　1.2.2 Identify customers

　　　1.2.3 Conduct market research

　1.3 Describe marketing strategy

　　　1.3.1 Describe objectives for strategy plan

　　　1.3.2 Identify marketing objectives

　　　1.3.3 Develop marketing strategy

　1.4 Edit marketing plan

　1.5 Publish marketing plan

Figure 39　Work Breakdown Structure of a Marketing Plan

References

General

Bliss, Edwin C. 1976. *Getting Things Done*. Toronto: Bantam Books.

Drucker, Peter F. 1974. *Management: Tasks, Responsibilities, Practices*. New York: Harper Calophon Books.

Gleeson, Keny. 1994. *The Personal Efficiency Program*. New York: John Wiley and Sons.

Scholtes, Peter R. 1998. *The Leader's Handbook*. New York: McGraw-Hill.

Senge, Peter M., Art Kleiner, Charlotte Roberts, Richard B. Ross, and Bryan J. Smith. 1994. *The Fifth Discipline Fieldbook*. New York: Doubleday.

Steward, Dorothy M. 1987. *Handbook of Management Skills*. London: Gower.

Creativity

Ayan, Jordan E. 1997. *Aha!: 10 Ways to Free Your Creative Spirit and Find Your Great Ideas*. New York: Crown Trade Paperbacks.

Buzan, Tony. 1993. *Use Both Sides of Your Brain*. New York: NAL/Dutton.

DeBono, Edward. 1994. *DeBono's Thinking Course*. New York: Facts on File, Inc.

———. 1991. *I Am Right—You Are Wrong*. New York: Penguin.

Forkes, Richard. 1993. *The Creative Problem Solver's Toolbox*. Corvalis, OR: Solutions Through Innovation.

Herrman, Ned. 1990. *The Creative Brain*. Luke Luce, NC: Brain Books.

Humphrey, Watts S. 1987. *Managing for Innovation*. Englewood Cliffs, NJ: Prentice Hall.

Williams, Linda V. 1983. *Teaching for the Two-Sided Mind*. New York: Touchstone.

Wonder, Jacqueline, and Priscilla Donovan. 1984. *Whole-Brain Thinking*. New York: Ballantine.

Information

Alessandra, Tony, and Phillip Hunsaker. 1993. *Communicating at Work*. New York: Simon and Schuster.

Arredondo, Lani. 1991. *How to Present Like a Pro*. New York: McGraw-Hill.

Axtell, Roger E. 1992. *Do's and Taboos of Public Speaking*. New York: John Wiley and Sons.

Beall, Melissa. 1991. *Guide to Oral Communications*. Dubuque, IA: Kendall-Hunt.

Booch, Grady. 1994. *Object-Oriented Analysis and Design with Applications*. Reading, MA: Addison-Wesley Publishing Co.

Booker, Dianna. 1994. *Communicate With Confidence*. New York: McGraw-Hill.

Borisoff, Deborah, and Michael Purdy, eds. 1991. *Listening in Everyday Life*. Lanham, MD: University Press of America.

Bozek, Phillip. 1994. *50 One-Minute Tips to Better Communication*. Menlo Park, CA: Crisp Publications.

Brock, Susan L. 1987. *Better Business Writing*. Menlo Park, CA: Crisp Publications.

Brockmann, R. John. 1990. *Writing Better Computer User Documentation*. New York: John Wiley and Sons.

Burley-Allen, Madelyn. 1995. *Listening: The Forgotten Skill*. New York: John Wiley and Sons.

Buzan, Tony. 1993. *Use Both Sides of Your Brain*. New York: NAL/Dutton.

Carnegie, Dale. 1990. *Quick and Easy Way to Effective Speaking*. New York: Pocket Books.

Coad, Peter, and Edward Yourdon. 1991. *Object-Oriented Analysis*. Englewood Cliffs, NJ: Prentice Hall.

DeMarco, Tom. 1979. *Structured Analysis and System Specifiction*. Englewood Cliffs, NJ: Prentice Hall, Inc.

Drake, John D. 1989. *The Effective Interviewer*. New York: AMACOM.

Gane, Chris, and Trish Sarson. 1979. *Structured Systems Analysis: Tools and Techniques*. Englewood Cliffs, NJ: Prentice Hall, Inc.

Hatley, Derke J., and Imtiaz Pirbhai. 1987. *A Strategies for Real-Time System Specification*. New York: Dorset House Publishing.

Heyman, Richard. 1994. *Why Didn't You Say That in the First Place?* San Francisco: Jossey-Bass.

Houghton-Alico, Joann. 1985. *Creating Computer Software Guides from Manuals to Menus*. New York: McGraw-Hill.

Jones, Meiler Page. 1996. *What Every Programmer Should Know about Object-Oriented Design*. New York: Dorset House.

Kliem, Ralph L. 1986. *Developing a Cost-Effective Company Operations Manual*. New York: Alexander Hamilton Institute.

Kliem, Ralph L., and Irwin S. Ludin. 1995. *Stand and Deliver: The Fine Art of Presentation*. Brookfield, VT: Ashgate.

Kupsh, Joyce, and Pat R. Graves. 1994. *How to Create High Impact Business Presentations*. Lincolnwood, IL: NTC Business Books.

Maggio, Rosalie. 1990. *How to Say It*. Englewood Cliffs, NJ: Prentice Hall.

Mendel, Steve. 1993. *Effective Presentation Skills*. Menlo Park, CA: Crisp Publications.

Ohmae, Kenichi. 1983. *The Mind of the Strategist*. New York: Penguin.

Rafe, Stephen C. 1991. *How to Be Prepared to Think on Your Feet and Make the Best Presentations of Your Life*. New York: Harper Collins.

Reid, James M., Jr. 1990. *Better Business Letters*. Reading, MA: Addison-Wesley.

Ross, Russell C. 1961. *Speak with Ease*. New York: Funk and Wagnalls.

Rumbaugh, James, et al. 1991. *Object-Oriented Modeling and Design*. Englewood Cliffs, NJ: Prentice Hall.

Siegel, Gerald. 1993. *Business and Professional Writing*. Dubuque, IA: Kendall/Hunt.

Wurman, Richard S. 1990. *Information Anxiety*. New York: Bantam Books.

Meetings

Daniels, William R. 1990. *Group Power II: A Manager's Guide to Conducting Regular Meetings*. Erlanger, KY: Pfeiffer and Co.

Doyle, David, and David Straus. 1982. *How to Make Meetings Work*. New York: Jove Books.

Glass, Robert L. 1988. *Software Communication Skills*. Englewood Cliffs, NJ: Prentice Hall.

Hawkins, Charlie. 1997. *First Aid for Meetings: Quick Fixes and Major Repairs for Running Effective Meetings*. Wilsonville, OR: Book Partners, Inc.

Levasseur, Robert E. 1994. *Breakthrough Business Meetings: Shared Leadership in Action*. Holbrook, MA: Adams Publishing.

Lippincott, Sharon M. 1994. *Meeting: Do's, Don'ts And Donuts: The Complete Handbook for Successful Meetings*. Pittsburgh, PA: Lighthouse Point Press.

Marshall, Jeanie. 1994. *Energetic Meetings: Enhancing Personal & Group Energy & Handling Difficult Behavior*. Santa Monica, CA: Jemel Publishing House.

Mosvick, Roger K., and Robert B. Nelson (contributor). 1996. *We've Got to Start Meeting Like This: A Guide to Successful Meeting Management*. Indianapolis, IN: Park Avenue.

Nadler, Leonard, and Zeace Nadler. 1987. *The Comprehensive Guide to Successful Conferences and Meetings*. San Francisco: Jossey-Bass.

Whitney, Dick, and Melissa Giovagnoli. 1997. *75 Cage-Rattling Questions to Change the Way You Work: Shake-Em-Up Questions to Open Meetings, Ignite Discussion, and Spark Creativity*. New York: McGraw-Hill.

Methods/Processes

Adair, James. 1989. *Problem Solving: A Top-Down Approach*. Glenview, IL: Scott, Foresman and Company.

Arnold, J. R. Tony. 1991. *Introduction to Materials Management*. Englewood Cliffs, NJ: Prentice Hall.

Arnold, John D. 1992. *The Complete Problem Solver*. New York: John Wiley and Sons.

Barr, John T. 1993. *SPC Tools for Everyone*. Milwaukee, WI: ASQC Quality Press.

Booch, Grady. 1994. *Object-Oriented Analysis and Design with Applications*. Reading, MA: Addison-Wesley Publishing Co.

Brunetti, Wayne H. 1993. *Achieving Total Quality*. White Plains, NY: Quality Resources.

Coad, Peter, and Edward Yourdon. 1991. *Object-Oriented Analysis*. Englewood Cliffs, NJ: Prentice Hall.

Cullen, Joe, and Jack Hollingum. 1987. *Implementing Total Quality*. London: IFS Limited.

DeMarco, Tom. 1979. *Structured Analysis and System Specifiction*. Englewood Cliffs, NJ: Prentice Hall, Inc.

Deming, W. Edwards. 1986. *Out of the Crisis*. Cambridge: Massachusetts Institute of Technology.

Gane, Chris, and Trish Sarson. 1979. *Structured Systems Analysis: Tools and Techniques*. Englewood Cliffs, NJ: Prentice Hall, Inc.

Gause, Donald C., and Gerald M. Weinberg. 1990. *Are Your Lights On?* New York: Dorset House.

Goddard, Walter E. 1986. *Just-in-Time: Surviving by Breaking Tradition*. Essex Junction, VT: Oliver Wight Publications, Inc.

Grady, Robert B., and Deborah L. Caswell. 1987. *Software Metrics*. Englewood Cliffs, NJ: Prentice Hall.

Grove, Andrew S. 1985. *High Output Management*. New York: Vintage Books.

Hammer, Michael, and James Champy. 1994. *Reengineering the Corporation*. New York: Harper Business.

Hatley, Derke J., and Imtiaz Pirbhai. 1987. *A Strategies for Real-Time System Specifiction*. New York: Dorset House Publishing.

Hunt, V. Daniel. 1993. *Reengineering*. Essex Junction, VT: Omneo.

Ishikawa, Kaoru. 1985. *What Is Total Quality Control?* Englewood Cliffs, NJ: Prentice Hall.

Jones, Meiler Page. 1996. *What Every Programmer Should Know about Object-Oriented Design*. New York: Dorset House.

Juran, J. M. 1989. *Juran on Leadership for Quality: An Executive Handbook*. New York: Free Press.

Kepner, Charles H., and Benjamin B. Tregoe. 1981. *The New Rational Manager*. Princeton, NJ: Princeton Research Press.

Kliem, Ralph L. 1990. *Managing the Modern Office*. Ramsey, NJ: Alexander Hamilton Institute.

Kliem, Ralph L., and Irwin S. Ludin. 1994. *Just-in-Time Systems for Computing Environments*. Westport, CT: Quorum Books.

Kliem, Ralph L., and Irwin S. Ludin. 1997. *Reducing Project Risk*. Brookfield, VT: Ashgate.

McNain, Carol J., and Kathleen H. J. Leibfried. 1994. *Benchmarking*. Essex Junction, VT: Oliver Wight Publications, Inc.

Niebel, Benjamin W. 1976. *Motion and Time Study*. Homewood, IL: Richard D. Irwin.

Rubin, Theodore. 1986. *Overcoming Indecisiveness*. New York: Avon Books.

Rumbaugh, James, et al. 1991. *Object-Oriented Modeling and Design*. Englewood Cliffs, NJ: Prentice Hall.

Sandras, William A. 1989. *Just-in-Time: Making It Happen*. New York: John Wiley and Sons.

Scherkenback, William W. 1991. *The Deming Route to Quality and Productivity*. Washington, DC: CEE Press Books.

Suzaki, Kiyoshi. 1987. *The New Manufacturing Challenge*. New York: Free Press.

Thomsett, Michael C. 1992. *Numberwise*. New York: AMACOM.

Walton, Mary. 1991. *Deming Management at Work*. New York: Perigee.

Wight, Oliver W. 1993. *The Executive's Guide to Successful MRPII*. Essex Junction, VT: Oliver Wight Publications, Inc.

Organization

Berlack, H. Robert. 1992. *Software Configuration Management*. New York: John Wiley and Sons.

Kliem, Ralph L. 1988. *AHI's Productivity Sourcebook*. New York: Alexander Hamilton Institute.

Landvater, Darryl V. 1993. *World Class Production and Inventory Management*. Essex Junction, VT: Oliver Wight Publications, Inc.

Latzko, William J., and David M. Saunders. 1995. *Four Days with Dr. Deming: A Strategy for Modern Methods of Management*. Reading, MA: Addison-Wesley.

Lubben, Richard T. 1988. *Just-in-Time Manufacturing*. New York: McGraw-Hill.

Mohrman, Susan Albers, Jay R. Galbraith, and Edward E. Lawler, III. 1998. *Tomorrow's Organization: Crafting Winning Capabilities in a Dynamic World*. San Francisco: Jossey-Bass.

Olson, Margaethe H., ed. 1989. *Technological Support for Work Group Collaboration*. Hillsdale, NJ: Lawrence Erlbaum Associates.

Pankoke-Babatz, Uta., ed. 1989. *Computer Based Group Communication*. Chickester: Ellis Harwood Limited.

Rye, David E. 1998. *1,001 Ways to Inspire: Your Organization, Your Team, and Yourself*. Franklin Lakes, NJ: Career Press.

Scott-Morgan, Peter B., and Arun Maira (contributor). 1996. *The Accelerating Organization: Embracing the Human Face of Change*. New York: McGraw-Hill.

People

Beckhard, Richard, and Wendy Pritchard. 1992. *Changing the Essence*. San Francisco: Jossey-Bass.

Bennis, Warren, and Burt Nanus. 1986. *Leaders: The Strategies for Taking Charge*. New York: Harperbusiness.

Block, Peter. 1993. *Stewardship*. San Francisco: Berrett-Koehler Publishers.

Block, Robert. 1983. *The Politics of Projects*. New York: Yourdon Press.

Bradford, David L., and Allan R. Cohen. 1984. *Managing for Excellence*. New York: John Wiley and Sons.

Bramson, Robert M. 1981. *Coping with Difficult People*. New York: Dell.

Carnegie, Dale, and Dorothy Carnegie. 1981. *How to Win Friends and Influence People*. New York: Simon and Schuster.

Cialdini, Robert B. 1993. *Influence: The Psychology of Persuasion*. New York: Morrow Press.

Covey, Stephen R. 1992. *Principle-Centered Leadership*. New York: Fireside.

Covey, Stephen R. 1990. *The Seven Habits of Highly Effective People*. New York: Fireside.

Dawson, Roger. 1992. *Secrets of Power Persuasion*. Englewood Cliffs, NJ: Prentice Hall.

Engel, Herbert M. 1983. *How to Delegate*. Houston, TX: Gulf Publishing Co.

Estess, Patricia S. 1996. *Work Concepts for the Future*. Menlo Park, CA: Crisp Publications.

Fisher, Roger, and William Ury. 1992. *Getting to Yes*. Boston: Houghton Mifflin.

Gato, Rex P. 1987. *Team Building and Communication*. Pittsburgh, PA: GTA Press.

James, Muriel, and Dorothy Jongeward (contributor). 1996. *Born to Win: Transactional Analysis with Gestalt Experiments*. Portland, OR: Perseus Press.

Jongerard, James. 1987. *Born to Win*. Reading, MA: Addison-Wesley.

Kanter, Rosabeth M. 1983. *The Change Masters*. New York: Simon and Schuster.

Kilman, Ralph, H., Teresa J. Covin, and Associates. 1988. *Corporate Transformation*. San Francisco: Jossey-Bass.

Kliem, Ralph L., and Irwin S. Ludin. 1995. *The People Side of Project Management*. Brookfield, VT: Ashgate.

Korizes, James M., and Barry Z. Posner. 1988. *The Leadership Challenge*. San Francisco: Jossey-Bass.

Marchington, Mick. 1992. *Managing the Team*. Cambridge, MA: Blackwell Publishers.

Mayer, Richard J. 1995. *Conflict Management*. Columbus, OH: Battelle Press.

Myers, Isabel Briggs, and Peter B. Myers (contributor). 1995. *Gifts Differing: Understanding Personality Type*. Palo Alto, CA: Consulting Psychologists Press.

Myers, Isabel Briggs. 1993. *Introduction to Type: A Guide to Understanding Your Results on the Myers-Briggs Type Indicator*. Gainesville, FL: Center for Applications of Psychological Type.

Nierenberg, Gerald I., and Henry H. Calero. 1981. *Meta Talk*. New York: Cornerstone Library.

Nirenberg, Jesse S. 1963. *Getting Through to People*. Englewood Cliffs, NJ: Prentice Hall.

Rees, Fran. 1991. *How to Lead Work Teams*. Erlanger, KY: Pfeiffer and Co.

Roberts, Wess. 1987. *Leadership Secrets of Attila the Hun*. New York: Warner Books.

Slaiken, Karl A. 1995. *When Push Comes to Shove*. San Francisco: Jossey-Bass.

Wierenberg, Gerald I. 1968. *The Art of Negotiating*. New York: Cornerstone Library.

Planning

Baker, Sunny, and Kim Baker. 1992. *On time/On Budget*. Englewood Cliffs, NJ: Prentice Hall.

Brimson, James A. 1991. *Activity Accounting*. New York: John Wiley and Sons.

DeMarco, Tom. 1982. *Controlling Software Projects*. Englewood Cliffs, NJ: Yourdon Press.

Edenborough, Robert. 1998. *Using Psychometrics: A Practical Guide to Testing and Assessment*. Dover, NH: Business Books Network.

Frame, J. Davidson. 1995. *Managing Projects in Organizations*. San Francisco: Jossey-Bass.

Frame, J. Davidson. 1995. *The New Project Management*. San Francisco: Jossey-Bass.

Graham, Robert J. 1989. *Project Management: As If People Mattered.* Bala Cynwyd, PA: Primavera Press.

Haynes, Marion E. 1989. *Project Management: From Idea to Implementation.* Menlo Park, CA: Crisp Publications.

Keane, Inc. 1995. *Productivity Management.* Boston: Keane, Inc.

Kliem, Ralph L. 1986. *The Secrets of Successful Project Management.* New York: John Wiley and Sons.

Kliem, Ralph L., Irwin S. Ludin, and Ken L. Robertson. 1997. *Practical Project Management Methodology.* New York: Marcel Dekker Sons.

Randolph, Alan, and Barry Z. Posner. 1991. *Getting the Job Done!* Englewood Cliffs, NJ: Prentice Hall.

Rouillard, Larrie. 1993. *Goals and Goal Setting.* Menlo Park, CA: Crisp Publications.

Whitten, Neal. 1990. *Managing Software Development Projects.* New York: John Wiley and Sons.

Time

Axelrod, Alan and Jim Holtje. 1997. *201 Ways to Manage Your Time Better (Quick-Tip Survival Guides).* New York: McGraw-Hill.

Barnes, Emilie. 1991. *The 15 Minute Organizer.* Eugene, OR: Harvest House Publishers.

Douglas, Merrill E., and Donna N. Douglas. 1993. *Manage Your Time, Your Work, Yourself.* New York: AMACOM.

Greissman, Eugene B. 1994. *Time Tactics of Very Successful People.* New York: McGraw-Hill.

Haynes, Marion E. 1991. *Practical Time Management.* Menlo Park, CA: Crisp Publications.

Lakein, Alan. 1990. *How to Get Control of Your Time and Your Life.* New York: NAL/Dutton.

MacKenzie, Alec. 1991. *The Time Trap.* New York: AMACOM.

Mayer, Jeffrey J. 1995. *Time Management for Dummies.* Foster City, CA: IDG Books Worldwide.

Pollar, Odette. 1996. *365 Ways to Simplify Your Work Life: Ideas That Bring More Time, Freedom, and Satisfaction to Daily Work.* Chicago: Financial Publications.

Timm, Paul R. 1993. *Successful Self-Management.* Menlo Park, CA: Crisp Publications.

Appendix

		CATEGORY							
TnT	Page #	Creativity	Information	Meetings	Methods/Processes	Organization	People	Planning	Time
Affinity Diagram	1		X		X				
Agenda	2			X		X		X	X
Analysis and Analysis Paralysis	3		X		X				
Authority	4					X	X		
Baselining	6		X		X			X	
Bell-Shaped Curve	7		X		X				
Benchmarking	9		X		X				
Brainstorming	10	X	X						
Breakeven Analysis	11		X		X				X
Cause-and-Effect Graph	13		X		X			X	
Chain of Command	15					X	X		
Change Control Sheet	16		X		X			X	
Change Management	18		X		X	X		X	
Charts and Graphs	19		X						
Checklists	20		X						
Checkpoint Review Meeting	21			X		X	X	X	
Chunking	22	X	X					X	
Communication Diagram	23		X				X		
Configuration Management	25				X			X	
Conflict Management	26			X		X	X		

		CATEGORY							
TnT	Page #	Creativity	Information	Meetings	Methods/Processes	Organization	People	Planning	Time
Consultant Selection	27					X	X		
Contingency Plan	28				X	X		X	
Contract Types	29		X					X	
Controlling	30		X		X	X			
Cost/Benefit Analysis	31		X		X				
Cost	32				X			X	
Crisis Management	33	X			X	X	X		X
Critical Issues/Action Items Log	34				X			X	
Critical Success Factors	35	X	X		X			X	
Daily Priority Task Listing	36							X	X
Data versus Information	37		X					X	
Decision-Making	38				X	X		X	
Decision Table	39		X		X				
Decision Tree	40		X		X				
Delegating	41	X				X	X		
Deming Wheel	42		X		X			X	
Design Principles	43	X			X	X			
Diagramming	44	X	X		X			X	
Document Templates	45	X	X		X			X	
Earned Value	47				X				

| | | CATEGORY | | | | | | | |
TnT	Page #	Creativity	Information	Meetings	Methods/Processes	Organization	People	Planning	Time
Efficiency and Effectiveness	49				X				
E-mail	50		X						
Entropy	51				X		X		
Equipment Usage Log	52		X		X			X	X
Facilitation (Workshops)	53			X					
Fishbone Diagram	54	X	X		X				
Five Ws	55	X	X		X		X	X	X
Flextime	56					X	X	X	X
Flowcharting	57	X	X		X			X	
Forms Layout	59	X	X		X			X	
Frequency Distribution	60		X		X			X	
Gantt Chart	62		X		X			X	X
Glossary	64		X					X	
Goals and Objectives	65							X	
Grouping	66	X	X					X	
Heuristics	68		X		X			X	
History File	69		X			X		X	
Hypothesis Formulation and Testing	70		X		X				
Imagineering	71	X							
Impact Analysis	72		X		X			X	

	CATEGORY							
TnT	Page #	Creativity	Information	Meetings	Methods/Processes	Organization	People	Planning	Time
Information Center	74	X	X			X		X	
Input-Process-Output Analysis Model	75	X	X		X				
Interruption Reduction	77	X			X		X		
Interviewing	78	X		X			X	X	
Issue-Action Diagram	79		X		X			X	
Just-in-Time Delivery	81					X			
Key Contact Listing	82		X	X			X	X	X
Leading	83	X					X		
Lessons Learned	84		X					X	
Listening	85	X	X	X	X		X	X	
Make-Buy Analysis	86							X	
Manufacturing Resource Planning (MRP II)	87					X			
Matrix	88	X	X		X			X	
Matrix versus Task Force Structure	89					X	X		
Mean	91		X		X				
Median	92		X		X				
Meetings	93		X	X		X	X	X	X
Memo of Understanding	94		X	X			X		
Methodology Development	95				X	X		X	
Metrics	96		X		X				

| | | CATEGORY | | | | | | | |
TnT	Page #	Creativity	Information	Meetings	Methods/Processes	Organization	People	Planning	Time
Mind Mapping	97	x	X						
Minutes	99		X	X			X		
Mode	100		X		X				
Modeling	101		X		X				
Myers-Briggs Type Indicator	102						X		
Negotiations	103	X	X		X		X		
Net Present Value	104				X			X	
Network Diagram	105							X	X
Newsletter	107		X						
No!	108						X	X	X
Nonmonetary Rewards	109	X					X	X	
Object versus Process Analysis	110		X		X				
Operations Manual	112		X		X	X			
Organization Chart	114		X			X	X		
Organizing	116			X	X	X	X		X
Outline	117	X	X						
Outsourcing	118					X	X		
Overcoming Bottlenecks	119	X			X				
P²M² Cycle	120	X			X	X		X	
Paradigms	122	X	X				X		

TnT	Page #	Creativity	Information	Meetings	Methods/Processes	Organization	People	Planning	Time
					CATEGORY				
Pareto Analysis	123		X		X			X	
Parkinson's Law	125								X
Participative Decision-Making	126	X	X	X	X	X	X		
Payback Analysis	128				X			X	
PERT Estimating Technique	130							X	X
Peter Principle	132					X	X		
Phase Breakdown	133	X			X			X	
Planning	135							X	
POSDCORB	136					X	X	X	
Presentations	137	X	X	X	X		X		
Priority Setting	138							X	
Probability	139		X		X			X	
Problem Analysis and Solution	140	X	X					X	
Procedures	141		X		X	X			
Process Streamlining	142	X			X			X	
Project Announcement	143							X	
Project Life Cycle	144					X		X	
Project Office	145		X	X		X	X	X	
Prototype	146	X			X			X	
Quality Review	147		X	X	X	X		X	

					CATEGORY				
TnT	Page #	Creativity	Information	Meetings	Methods/ Processes	Organization	People	Planning	Time
Quartiles	149		X		X				
Recycle and Resale	150	X			X			X	
Reengineering	151	X			X	X			
Replanning	152							X	
Reports	153	X	X	X		X		X	
Request for Proposal (Response)	154		X		X				
Resource Leveling	155				X		X	X	
Responsibility Matrix	157				X	X	X	X	
Return on Investment	158							X	
Reuse	160	X	X		X	X		X	
Risk Management	161				X			X	
Sampling	163		X		X				
Scattergram	164	X	X		X				
Scientific Method	166		X		X				
S Curve	167							X	
Self-Directed Work Teams	169					X	X		
Single Point of Contact	170					X	X		
Sketch	171	X	X					X	
Software Selection	172				X				
Span of Control	173					X	X		X

		CATEGORY							
TnT	Page #	Creativity	Information	Meetings	Methods/ Processes	Organization	People	Planning	Time
Speed-Reading	174								X
Staff Meetings	175			X		X	X	X	
Standards	176		X		X	X		X	
Statement of Work (Understanding)	177							X	
Statistical Corruptions and Distortions	178		X		X				
Statistical Process Control Chart	179		X		X				
Status Collection	181		X		X				
Status Review Meetings	183		X	X	X	X	X	X	
Supply Chain Manufacturing	184					X			
SWAT Teams	185				X	X	X		
Systems Theory	186				X	X			
T Account Decision-Making	187							X	
Teamwork	189	X		X		X	X		
Telecommuting	190					X			
Telephone Tag	191	X	X		X		X		
Testing	192				X				
Time Log	193		X		X			X	
Total Quality Management	195	X			X				
Transactional Analysis	196						X		
Transportation Consolidation	197	X			X	X		X	X

		CATEGORY							
TnT	Page #	Creativity	Information	Meetings	Methods/Processes	Organization	People	Planning	Time
Unity of Command	198					X	X		
Validity Threats	199		X		X				
Value Management	200							X	
Variability	201		X		X				
Verification	202		X		X				
Videoconferencing	203		X	X					
Viewfoils	204	X	X	X					
Virtual Teams	205					X	X		
Visibility Wall/Room	206	X	X	X		X	X	X	
Web Site	207		X		X				
Weighted Selection Criteria Approach	208				X				
Work Breakdown Structure	210				X				

UPGRADE YOUR PROJECT MANAGEMENT KNOWLEDGE WITH FIRST-CLASS PUBLICATIONS FROM PMI

PROJECT MANAGEMENT SOFTWARE SURVEY

The PMI® *Project Management Software Survey* offers an efficient way to compare and contrast the capabilities of a wide variety of project management tools. More than two hundred software tools are listed with comprehensive information on systems features, how they perform time analysis, resource analysis, cost analysis, performance analysis, and cost reporting, and how they handle multiple projects, project tracking, charting, and much more. The survey is a valuable tool to help narrow the field when selecting the best project management tools. ISBN: 1-880410-52-4 (paperback), ISBN: 1-880410-59-1 (CD-ROM)

SUCCESSFUL INFORMATION SYSTEM IMPLEMENTATION, SECOND EDITION

Successful implementation of information systems technology lies in managing the behavioral and organizational components of the process. Past data on this subject has involved mostly case studies, but this book provides practical information those implementing information systems can use now. Pinto and Millet offer practical information on "approaching the subject from a managerial, rather than a technical, perspective." The second edition of this work covers such topics as implementation theory, prioritizing projects, implementation success and failure, critical success factors, and more! ISBN: 1-880410-66-4 (paperback)

RECIPES FOR PROJECT SUCCESS

This book is destined to become *the* reference book for beginning project managers, particularly those who like to cook! Practical, logically developed project management concepts are offered in easily understood terms in a lighthearted manner. They are applied to the everyday task of cooking—from simple, single dishes, such as homemade tomato sauce for pasta, made from the bottom up, to increasingly complex dishes or meals for groups that in turn require an understanding of more complex project management terms and techniques. The transistion between cooking and project management discussions is smooth, and tidbits of information provided with the recipes are interesting and humorous. ISBN: 1-880410-58-3 (paperback)

THE FUTURE OF PROJECT MANAGEMENT

The project management profession is going through tremendous change—both evolutionary and revolutionary. Some of these changes are internally driven while many are externally driven. Here, for the first time, is a composite view of some major trends occurring throughout the world and the implication of them on the profession of project management and on the Project Management Institute. Read the views of the 1998 PMI Research Program Team, a well-respected futurist firm and other authors. This book represents the beginning of a journey and through inputs from readers and others, it will continue as a work in progress.
ISBN: 1-880410-71-0 (paperback)

THE JUGGLER'S GUIDE TO MANAGING MULTIPLE PROJECTS

This comprehensive book introduces and explains task-oriented, independent, and interdependent levels of project portfolios. It says that you must first have a strong foundation in time management and priority setting, then introduces the concept of Portfolio Management to timeline multiple projects, determine their resource requirements, and handle emergencies, putting you in charge for possibly the first time in your life!
ISBN: 1-880410-65-6 (paperback)

NEW RESOURCES FOR PMP CANDIDATES

The following publications are resources that certification candidates can use to gain information on project management theory, principles, techniques, and procedures.

PMP RESOURCE PACKAGE

Earned Value Project Management
        by Quentin W. Fleming and Joel M. Koppelman
Effective Project Management: How to Plan, Manage, and Deliver Projects on Time and Within Budget
        by Robert K. Wysocki, et al.
A Guide to the Project Management Body of Knowledge (PMBOK™ Guide)
        by the PMI Standards Committee
Human Resource Skills for the Project Manager
        by Vijay K. Verma
The New Project Management
        by J. Davidson Frame
Organizing Projects for Success
        by Vijay K. Verma
Principles of Project Management
        by John Adams, et al.
Project & Program Risk Management
        by R. Max Wideman, Editor
Project Management Casebook
        edited by David I. Cleland, et al.
Project Management: A Managerial Approach, Third Edition
        by Jack R. Meredith and Samuel J. Mantel, Jr.
Project Management: A Systems Approach to Planning, Scheduling, and Controlling, Sixth Edition
        by Harold Kerzner

A Guide to the Project Management Body of Knowledge (PMBOK™ Guide)

The basic management reference for everyone who works on projects. Serves as a tool for learning about the generally accepted knowledge and practices of the profession. As "management by projects" becomes more and more a recommended business practice worldwide, the *PMBOK™ Guide* becomes an essential source of information that should be on every manager's bookshelf. Available in hardcover or paperback, the *PMBOK™ Guide* is an official standards document of the Project Management Institute.
ISBN: 1-880410-12-5 (paperback), ISBN: 1-880410-13-3 (hardcover)

Interactive PMBOK Guide

This CD-ROM makes it easy for you to access the valuable information in PMI's *PMBOK™ Guide*. Features hypertext links for easy reference—simply click on underlined words in the text, and the software will take you to that particular section in the *PMBOK™ Guide*. Minimum system requirements: 486 PC; 8MB RAM; 10MB free disk space; CD-ROM drive; mouse, or other pointing device; and Windows 3.1 or greater.

Managing Projects Step-by-Step™

Follow the steps, standards, and procedures used and proven by thousands of professional project managers and leading corporations. This interactive multimedia CD-ROM based on PMI's *PMBOK™ Guide* will enable you to customize, standardize, and distribute your project plan standards, procedures, and methodology across your entire organization. Multimedia illustrations using 3-D animations and audio make this perfect for both self-paced training or for use by a facilitator.

PMBOK™ Q&A

Use this handy pocket-sized question-and-answer study guide to learn more about the key themes and concepts presented in PMI's international standard, *PMBOK™ Guide*. More than 160 multiple-choice questions with answers (referenced to the *PMBOK™ Guide*) help you with the breadth of knowledge needed to understand key project management concepts.
ISBN: 1-880410-21-4 (paperback)

PMI Proceedings Library CD-ROM

This interactive guide to PMI's annual Seminars & Symposium proceedings offers a powerful new option to the traditional methods of document storage and retrieval, research, training, and technical writing. Contains complete paper presentations from PMI '92–PMI '97 with full-text search capability, convenient onscreen readability, and PC/Mac compatibility.

PMI Publications Library CD-ROM

Using state-of-the-art technology, PMI offers complete articles and information from its major publications on one CD-ROM, including *PM Network* (1990–97), *Project Management Journal* (1990–97), and *A Guide to the Project Management Body of Knowledge*. Offers full-text search capability and indexing by *PMBOK™ Guide* knowledge areas. Electronic indexing schemes and sophisticated search engines help to find and retrieve articles quickly that are relevant to your topic or research area.

ALSO AVAILABLE FROM PMI

Project Management for Managers
Mihály Görög, Nigel J. Smith
ISBN: 1-880410-54-0 (paperback)

Project Leadership: From Theory to Practice
Jeffery K. Pinto, Peg Thoms, Jeffrey Trailer, Todd Palmer, Michele Govekar
ISBN: 1-880410-10-9 (paperback)

Annotated Bibliography of Project and Team Management
David I. Cleland, Gary Rafe, Jeffrey Mosher
ISBN: 1-880410-47-8 (paperback),
ISBN: 1-880410-57-5 (CD-ROM)

How to Turn Computer Problems into Competitive Advantage
Tom Ingram
ISBN: 1-880410-08-7 (paperback)

Achieving the Promise of Information Technology
Ralph B. Sackman
ISBN: 1-880410-03-6 (paperback)

Leadership Skills for Project Managers
Editors' Choice Series
Edited by Jeffrey K. Pinto, Jeffrey W. Trailer
ISBN: 1-880410-49-4 (paperback)

The Virtual Edge
Margery Mayer
ISBN: 1-880410-16-8 (paperback)

ABCs of DPC
Edited by PMI's Design-Procurement-Construction Specific Interest Group
ISBN: 1-880410-07-9 (paperback)

Project Management Casebook
Edited by David I. Cleland, Karen M. Bursic, Richard Puerzer, A. Yaroslav Vlasak
ISBN: 1-880410-45-1 (paperback)

Project Management Casebook Instructor's Manual
Edited by David I. Cleland, Karen M. Bursic, Richard Puerzer, A. Yaroslav Vlasak
ISBN: 1-880410-18-4 (paperback)

PMI Book of Project Management Forms
ISBN: 1-880410-31-1 (paperback)
ISBN: 1-880410-50-8 (diskette version 1.0)

Principles of Project Management
John Adams et al.
ISBN: 1-880410-30-3 (paperback)

Organizing Projects for Success
Human Aspects of Project Management Series, Volume 1, Vijay K. Verma
ISBN: 1-880410-40-0 (paperback)

Human Resource Skills for the Project Manager
Human Aspects of Project Management Series, Volume 2, Vijay K. Verma
ISBN: 1-880410-41-9 (paperback)

Managing the Project Team
Human Aspects of Project Management Series, Volume 3, Vijay K. Verma
ISBN: 1-880410-42-7 (paperback)

Earned Value Project Management
Quentin W. Fleming, Joel M. Koppelman
ISBN: 1-880410-38-9 (paperback)

Value Management Practice
Michel Thiry
ISBN: 1-880410-14-1 (paperback)

Decision Analysis in Projects
John R. Schuyler
ISBN: 1-880410-39-7 (paperback)

The World's Greatest Project
Russell W. Darnall
ISBN: 1-880410-46-X (paperback)

Power & Politics in Project Management
Jeffrey K. Pinto
ISBN: 1-880410-43-5 (paperback)

Best Practices of Project Management Groups in Large Functional Organizations
Frank Toney, Ray Powers
ISBN: 1-880410-05-2 (paperback)

Project Management in Russia
Vladimir I. Voropajev
ISBN: 1-880410-02-8 (paperback)

A Framework for Project and Program Management Integration
R. Max Wideman
ISBN: 1-880410-01-X (paperback)

Quality Management for Projects & Programs
Lewis R. Ireland
ISBN: 1-880410-11-7 (paperback)

Project & Program Risk Management
Edited by R. Max Wideman
ISBN: 1-880410-06-0 (paperback)

ORDER ONLINE AT WWW.PMIBOOKSTORE.ORG

Book Ordering Information
Phone: 412.741.6206
Fax: 412.741.0609
Email: pmiorders@abdintl.com
Mail: PMI Publications Fulfillment Center,
    PO Box 1020,
    Sewickley, Pennsylvania 15056-1304 USA